HUGH CARPENTER & TERI SANDISON

Hot Barbecue

TEN SPEED PRESS

Berkeley, California

TEN SPEED PRESS
Post Office Box 7123
Berkeley, California 94707
www.tenspeed.com

Distributed in Australia by Simon & Schuster Australia, in Canada by Ten Speed Press Canada,
in New Zealand by Tandem Press, in South Africa by Real Books, in Southeast Asia by Berkeley
Books, and in the United Kingdom and Europe by Airlift Books.

Cover and book design by Beverly Wilson.
Typography by Scott Woodworth.
Typefaces used in this book are Avant Garde, Futura, and Van Dijk.

Library of Congress CIP Data
Carpenter, Hugh
Hot Barbecue/Hugh Carpenter and Teri Sandison
     p.   cm.
Includes index.
ISBN 0-89815-900-8
1. Barbecue cookery   I. Sandison, Teri   II. Title.
TX840.B3C33   1996
641.7'6–dc21   96-36818
                         CIP

Printed in Hong Kong
First printing, 1997

4 5 6 7 8 9 10 — 02 01 00 99

To Lorenzo and Patricia Dall'Armi, who gather

their family and friends around the dining table nightly for

wonderful food, great wines, and special friendships.

Thanks so much for enriching

our lives in many ways.

Contents

Hot Barbecue Night After Night

Webster's Unabridged Dictionary: bar'be cue, n. (Sp. barbacoa, from Haitian barbacoa, a framework of sticks.) 1. originally, a framework to hold meat over a fire to be smoked, dried, or broiled. 2. any meat broiled or roasted on a spit over an open fire. 3. an entertainment, usually outdoors, at which such meat is prepared and eaten.

Whether you are barbecuing on the balcony of a high-rise apartment, covering seafood with layers of seaweed and hot rocks for a New England clambake, pit-smoking a whole pig on a sultry Tennessee night, or cooking hamburgers on a high-tech Weber Genesis grill, no other word captures such diverse culinary and social activity, nor does any other cooking technique have such deep national roots.

The word barbecue is controversial. In this book we follow Webster's general definition that a barbecue is a social activity involving cooking food over direct heat or by slow-smoking the food in a closed container at low temperatures. Many Southern cooks use the word barbecue to mean only tough cuts of meat that have been slow-cooked for hours until the meat becomes marvelously flavorful and succulent. To these cooks and most chefs, cooking food over direct fire is "grilling." Yet even within the South there is strong disagreement about what constitutes "true barbecue." North Carolinians brush pork with a thin vinegar sauce, but just one state away in South Carolina barbecue is meat basted with a mustard sauce. Tennesseans barbecue pork in a pit, and if you tell Georgian cooks about a Texan barbecued beef brisket glazed with spicy tomato sauce, they'll shake their heads in disbelief. So, we just invite friends over for "a barbecue," have a good time, and let the experts debate the proper definition of the word.

One of the earliest references to the word barbecue is found in Samuel Johnson's dictionary. He writes, "To Barbecue. A term used in the West-Indies for dressing a hog whole; which, being split to the back-bone, is laid flat upon a large gridiron, raised about two foot above a charcoal fire, with which it is surrounded." As a social event, barbecue was described in Philip Fithian's 1774 journals: "I was invited this morning by Captain Fibbs to a barbecue; this differs but little from the fish feasts; instead of fish the dinner is roasted pig, with the proper appendages, but the diversions & exercise are the same as both."

Barbecue has made the outdoors our "great room" for congenial social activity. In 1995 Americans fired up their grills more than 2.6 billion times. Over 75 percent of households own a grill, with grill ownership split evenly between charcoal and gas grills. Increasing numbers of cooks are buying grills with larger cooking surfaces, shelves, side burners, fuel gauges, and grease catchers. Interest in smoke-cooking has escalated, with nearly twice as many people, 9 percent, owning smokers as four years ago. In a recent survey by the National Barbecue Association, cooks cited as their reasons for barbecuing: great flavor (91 percent), pleasant to be outside (73 percent), change of pace (67 percent), easy cleanup (61 percent), and informality (59 percent). Just fifteen years ago barbecue equipment was sold only at hardware stores. Today, nearly every city has stores that specialize in barbecue equipment and the ever-increasing range of barbecue cooking accessories.

We barbecue several nights a week. It is the easiest way to create complex-tasting food with a minimum of preparation time. Barbecuing over direct heat sears and traps the juices, browns the exterior, concentrates and caramelizes the marinade, and infuses food with unique smoky essences. Slow-smoking flavors food with a subtle smoky flavor and during the long cooking process transforms the toughest cuts of meat into succulent, tender taste sensations. The resulting layers of flavor make barbecuing over direct heat and slow-smoking a perfect choice for everyday dinners and festive occasions. Gather your family and friends, open some icy drinks, fire up the heat, prod the food knowingly while making sage remarks, and enjoy this great outdoor cooking sport.

Hugh Carpenter and Teri Sandison

Hot Grilling Techniques

The essential equipment for grilling is not the grill, it's the griller. The best grill chefs hover over the fire, baby the food, and share their thoughts about the theory, practice, and mysteries of grilling to all who approach their cooking sanctum.

- Always build a larger fire than you think necessary so that the coals do not burn out before the food finishes cooking. The area of the spread-out coals should be 2 to 4 inches beyond the food.

- When cooking over briquettes, lump hardwood, or wood, plan ahead. Briquettes will be ash covered in about 20 minutes. Lump hardwood, which burns much hotter, will take about 30 to 40 minutes to reach the gray-ash stage. If you add the food before this stage, the intense heat will burn the food, and if the briquettes are still partly black, the heat will be uneven.

- Once the fire is lighted, spread the coals into an even layer. When using a kettle grill, instead of positioning the coals with long tongs, hold the grill by the handle and give it a little shake to distribute the coals.

- Once the coals are covered with ash and are evenly distributed, position the cooking rack over the coals. Let the rack become very hot. If the cooking rack is not clean, brush it vigorously to remove all food and carbon residue from the previous grilling session. Alternatively, as soon as you remove the food from the rack, scrub the rack with a wire brush.

- To prevent food from sticking, brush the cooking rack with flavorless cooking oil. Never use nonstick cooking spray.

- It is better to err with heat that is too low rather than too high. If cooking over briquettes, lump hardwood charcoal, or wood, control the heat by opening and closing the vents. If the heat is too high, cover the grill and partially close the vents. This reduces the amount of oxygen feeding the fire, and the intensity of the heat will be reduced quickly. For more about this, see "Laying and Starting the Fire," page 65.

- To add an intense flavor to grilled meat and seafood, add hardwood chips, oak bark, or barrel staves. This is an especially useful technique for gas grills, because gas flames and vaporizing slats or lava rocks do not create the intense flavor that briquettes, lump hardwood charcoal, and wood do. Wood chips are available at supermarkets and hardware stores. Soak approximately 1 cup of chips in cold water to cover for 30 minutes, then drain. Scatter the chips over the charcoal just before adding the food. On gas grills, remove the cooking rack. Turn the gas jets on. Place the chips on a layer of aluminum foil and position this on the metal vaporizing slats or on the lava rocks at one corner of the fuel bed. Reposition the cooking rack. Wait until the wood begins to smoke, place the food on the rack, and cover with the lid. (Caution: if there is any danger of the foil holding the chips extinguishing the gas flames, then place it on the cooking rack instead.) Other flavor options include adding rosemary sprigs, whole walnuts crushed with a hammer and soaked in cold water, unpeeled garlic cloves, cinnamon sticks and whole nutmegs, and citrus peels.

● Most foods should be grilled over medium heat. Place your open hand, palm side down, 4 inches above the heat, and count "1001, 1002, 1003." The heat is medium if it's hot enough to make you pull your hand away at "1003." While most gas barbecues come with a built-in thermometer, we find that the hand technique is a more accurate way to judge temperature.

● Food should be at room temperature so that it cooks more quickly and evenly.

● Don't overcrowd the grill so that the food touches. It's important that the heat rise around the sides of the food.

● If flare-ups occur due to fat dripping from the meat and/or because of oil in the marinade, spray the fire with a water spritzer.

● Turn food frequently. It's better to turn food too often than to wait too long and discover that it has burned on the underside.

● Grill most foods with the grill covered. The exceptions are boneless chicken breasts, shrimp, very thin steaks, vegetables, and skewered foods. These foods must be rotated often and cook so quickly that they need constant attention.

The Direct Method: With foods of varying thicknesses, such as chicken pieces, place the thicker pieces over the hottest part of the fire, or begin cooking them a few minutes earlier, or once they are cooked, transfer the pieces to the cooler edges of the cooking rack.

The Indirect Method: Grill large pieces of meat such as whole game hens, chickens, and turkeys by the indirect method. Light the coals and, when they are ash covered, push the coals to the sides of the fuel bed. Place a small disposable aluminum pan in the center of the fuel bed, add the cooking rack, brush the cooking rack with oil, then position the meat over the drip pan. Approximately every 30 minutes, add about 14 new briquettes or lumps of hardwood charcoal so that a constant, even heat is maintained. Many barbecue chefs like to light these coals in a small disposable aluminum tray, then transfer lit coals to the grill. For gas grills whose burners can be individually controlled, keep the outside burners on low and the middle burner off.

Defining the Terms

arbecue As described by Webster's dictionary, a social activity involving cooking food over direct heat or by slow-smoking in a sealed container at low heat.

Grilling: Cooking over direct or indirect heat, usually from 350° to 500°. Grilling is ideal for cooking all firm-fleshed fish; shellfish; tender cuts of meat of various sizes such as chicken either whole or cut into pieces, pork loin and tenderloin, beef fillet and steaks and butterflied leg of lamb; and a wide range of vegetables.

Slow-Smoking: Cooking in a covered container in which heat is maintained at a 200° to 220° range throughout the long cooking process. Slow smoking is used for tough cuts of meat such as beef briskets, shanks, pork butt, and spareribs because the very long, slow cooking process transforms tough meat to an incredible succulent tenderness. This technique can also be used for cooking firm-fleshed fish, shellfish, poultry, and tender cuts of meat when you want the food to acquire a smoky flavor.

Indirect Heat: A technique used to grill large pieces of meat such as whole chickens and turkeys so that they do not burn. The meat is placed on the cooking rack over a drip pan and coals are spread around the edges of the fuel bed. The heat is maintained at 350°, and more coals are added periodically.

Direct Heat: This is the most common technique for grilling firm-fleshed fish, shellfish, tender meats, and vegetables. Foods are placed on the grill and cooked over direct heat, whether the fuel is briquettes, lump hardwood charcoal, wood, or gas.

Brines and Dry Cures: Brines, or wet cures, are marinades with a large amount of salt. They are used to change the texture and moisture content of food being readied for the grill or smoker. Brining can last from 1 to 24 hours. It is most commonly used as a preparation technique for tough cuts of meat that are to be smoked. Dry cures are combinations of salt, sugar, and spices that are rubbed over meat and seafood and are used for the same purpose as brines.

Dry Rubs: Combinations of dry ingredients such as dried herbs, ground spices, sugar, and salt that are rubbed into food prior to cooking. If the mixture contains a large amount of salt, it is a dry cure.

Pastes, or Slathers: Pastes, or slathers, are similar to dry rubs except that the seasonings and spices are bound together into a thick mixture by a liquid ingredient such as prepared mustard, hoisin sauce, or peanut butter.

Marinades: A liquid used to tenderize and flavor food. The marinating process can last from just minutes to hours. If the marinade contains a large amount of salt, then it is a brine.

Mops: Any liquid that is brushed on food being grilled or smoked. A mop can be a marinade, or a special seasoning combination ranging from a vinegar mix to melted butter, or it can be a barbecue sauce.

Sops: Any liquid that is served on a plate next to grilled or smoked food. Sop up the liquid with the meat or seafood.

Barbecue Sauces: These thick, rich-tasting sauces are used as a mop during cooking, or brushed over the food after it has been cooked, or as a sop.

A Note on Marinades

Many of the marinades in this book can be made in larger quantities and stored indefinitely in the refrigerator. This includes marinades that contain vinegar, all the Asian bottled condiments, minced ginger, garlic, and the minced zest of citrus. The exceptions are marinades that contain citrus juice and/or fresh herbs and green onions, which deteriorate very quickly if stored for more than 1 day, even if refrigerated. When making large amounts of marinades that contain these ingredients, omit the citrus and/or herbs, and store the marinade in a glass container in the refrigerator. On the container, place a sticker that indicates the amount of freshly squeezed citrus juice and/or fresh herbs to add for every cup of marinade. Once you have added the citrus juice and/or fresh herbs, use that portion of the marinade that day or discard.

Grilled and Smoked Seafood Triumphs

Grilling and smoking are wonderful choices for cooking nearly all types of fish and shellfish. With just a few minutes of preliminary marinating and a little attention during cooking, seafood acquires an unrivaled flavor. Perfectly grilled seafood has its natural flavor accented, marinades add their own complex tastes, the smoky essences cling to the exterior, and the flesh retains its incredible moistness. Smoking seafood, while taking longer than grilling, produces extraordinarily tender flesh with an alluring smoky flavor. Whether you grill or slow-smoke seafood, these recipes will make even those who aren't seafood enthusiasts ask for second helpings.

Fish: Practically all types of fish can be grilled or smoked except fillet of sole, which quickly disintegrates during cooking. Swordfish: does not need to be marinated; just rub it with a little oil and place it on the grill over direct heat. Shark, Tuna, Mahimahi, Salmon Steaks, and Halibut Steaks: marinate and place on the grill over direct heat. Salmon Fillets: marinate, then lay the fillet skin side down over direct heat, cover, and cook until the flesh begins to flake; do not turn the fillet over. Fillets of Snapper, Halibut, Catfish, Sea Bass: all fish that flakes easily should be placed on a grill pan that has been preheated on the grill, or on a double layer of heavy duty aluminum foil. Sand Dabs and Trout: These and other small whole fish, whether boned or not, can be laid on the grill and cooked over direct heat.

Shellfish: Shrimp: Use medium to large shrimp and cook over direct heat until the center of the flesh turns white. Sea Scallops: if the grating is close together, cook over direct heat, or preheat a grill pan and then cook the scallops on the grill. The scallops are done when they just lose their raw color in the center (cut into one). Soft-Shell Crab: place on the grill over direct heat, and brush with a marinade; cook on both sides until the crabs turn red. Live Lobster: drop live lobsters into a large pot of boiling water and cook for 3 minutes; then remove, split them in half, brush with a marinade or melted butter, and cook shell down over direct heat until the lobster meat turns completely white. Squid: Clean the squid; then cook on a grill pan that has been preheated on the grill; the squid are done when they turn white. Oysters, Mussels, and Clams: place these over direct heat; as they begin to open, brush with seasoned melted butter, a marinade, or a mop; cook 1 more minute and then serve.

Points to Remember with Grilling Fish and Shellfish

- Always use the freshest seafood, and in particular, never buy frozen fish for grilling or smoking. Very fresh fish will have a beautiful glossy sheen that is entirely absent from fish that has been removed from the water for several days or frozen and thawed.

- Fish is highly absorbent. Marinate for 5 minutes, but not longer than 30 minutes. Longer marinating can cause the flesh to deteriorate and become mushy.

- For safety reasons, never brush any marinade over fish or shellfish during the last five minutes of grilling. You can reserve a little of the marinade prior to marinating, and then spoon this over the cooked fish or shellfish after it is transferred to dinner plates. (The exception to this rule is bivalves such as mussels, which are not brushed with a marinade until they open, at which point they are already cooked).

- Grill most fish and shellfish over medium heat. One exception is tuna which is better seared over medium high heat.

- Most fish is perfectly cooked when the flesh just begins to flake when prodded with a fork and knife. Tuna is the exception. It should be served when the interior meat is still raw to medium-rare.

- To turn fish steaks and fillets over, place one hand across the top of the fish (this side will not have been cooked and so will be cool), slide a spatula under the fish, and then support the fish with your hand as you carefully turn it over.

- When cooking large shrimp, use scissors to cut the shell along the back, then work the marinade under the shell. Now when you grill the shrimp, the shell will protect it from becoming dry, and the marinade will soak into the shrimp. Or shell and butterfly the shrimp, then brush the shrimp with the marinade or melted butter during grilling.

- An easy method for cooking sea scallops is to run two skewers through a scallop, and then add more scallops onto the double skewer until it is filled. Now it is easy to turn the scallops over, and none of the scallops will be able to rotate around the skewers.

This glaze, which is excellent on all fish, poultry, game, pork, and veal, has many variations. Try replacing the lime zest and juice with lemon, using fresh basil or mint as an addition to, or in place of, the cilantro, or adding 1/4 cup finely minced fresh ginger. However, because the citrus juice deteriorates quickly, use the marinade the day it is made. As a possible menu, accompany this dish with barbecued corn, jicama salad, and apricot crisp.

Swordfish with Asian Sweet and Sour Citrus Glaze *excellent*

— Serves 4 as an entrée

INGREDIENTS

2 pounds fresh swordfish, about 1 inch thick

Flavorless cooking oil to brush on the cooking rack

ASIAN SWEET & SOUR CITRUS GLAZE

¼ cup Chinese rice wine or dry sherry

¼ cup oyster sauce

¼ cup honey

Finely minced zest of 1 lime

¼ cup freshly squeezed lime juice

½ teaspoon Asian chile sauce

4 cloves garlic, finely minced

¼ cup chopped cilantro sprigs

¼ cup minced green onion

ADVANCE PREPARATION

Place the swordfish in a nonreactive container, cover, and refrigerate. Set aside the cooking oil, if grilling. In a small bowl, combine the glaze ingredients and mix well. If not using right away, cover and refrigerate. *All advance preparation may be completed up to 8 hours before you begin the final steps.*

FINAL STEPS

At least 10 minutes but not more than 30 minutes in advance of cooking, pour the glaze over the swordfish. Turn the swordfish over so that it is evenly coated. Keep refrigerated.

To Grill: If using a gas or electric grill, preheat to medium (350°). If using charcoal or wood, prepare a fire. When the gas or electric grill is preheated or the coals or wood are ash covered, brush the cooking rack with the oil, then lay the swordfish in the center of the rack. Regulate the heat so that it remains at a medium temperature. Grill for about 4 minutes on each side, brushing on more of the marinade. The swordfish is done when it just begins to flake when prodded with a knife and fork.

To Smoke: Bring the fish to room temperature, about 15 minutes. Prepare the smoker for barbecuing, bringing the temperature to 200° to 220°. Smoke the swordfish for about 45 minutes, or until it just begins to flake. During smoking, brush on more of the marinade.

To Broil: Preheat the broiler. Place the swordfish 4 inches from the heat source and cook it until the swordfish just begins to flake. During broiling, brush on more of the marinade.

To Serve: Transfer the fish to a heated serving platter or 4 heated dinner plates and serve at once.

Balsamic vinegar, with its slightly sweet, mildly acidic, and complex woody essence, is one of the great flavor enhancers. Produced in northern Italy in the area of Modena, balsamic vinegar is a reduction of white Trebbiano grape juice that is aged in wood barrels traditionally stored in farmhouse attics for decades. Such true balsamic vinegar, which is both very expensive and difficult to find in this country, is usually sprinkled sparingly on food. For this recipe we use inexpensive balsamic vinegar as a flavor foundation for a sweet and sour herb-scented sauce. As a possible menu, accompany this dish with pasta tossed with Parmesan and pepper; buttered peas; and a peach tart.

Swordfish with Balsamic Essence *excellent*

Serves 4 as an entree

INGREDIENTS

2 pounds fresh swordfish, about 1 inch thick

Flavorless cooking oil to brush on the cooking rack

¼ cup cilantro sprigs

2 tablespoons unsalted butter, at room temperature

1 tablespoon flavorless cooking oil

1 tablespoon very finely minced ginger

BALSAMIC ESSENCE

7 tablespoons balsamic vinegar

3 tablespoons sugar

2 tablespoons thin soy sauce

2 tablespoons minced green onion

1½ teaspoons cornstarch

½ teaspoon Asian chile sauce

½ teaspoon salt

ADVANCE PREPARATION

Place the swordfish in a nonreactive container, cover, and refrigerate. In separate containers, set aside the cilantro and butter. Combine the cooking oil and ginger and set aside. In a small bowl, combine all ingredients of the balsamic essence. If not using right away, then refrigerate. *All advance preparation may be completed up to 8 hours before you begin the final steps.*

FINAL COOKING STEPS

Mince the cilantro, and set aside.

To Grill: If using a gas or electric grill, preheat to medium (350°). If using charcoal or wood, prepare a fire. When the gas or electric grill is preheated or the coals or wood are ash covered, brush the cooking rack with oil, then lay the swordfish in the center of the rack. Regulate the heat so that it remains at a medium temperature. Grill the fish for about 4 minutes on each side. The swordfish is done when it just begins to flake when prodded with a knife and fork.

To Smoke: Bring the fish to room temperature, about 15 minutes. Prepare the smoker for barbecuing, bringing the temperature to 200° to 220°. Smoke the swordfish about 45 minutes until it just begins to flake.

To Broil: Preheat the broiler. Place the swordfish 4 inches from the broiler heat source and cook until it just begins to flake.

To Serve: Transfer to a heated serving platter or 4 heated dinner plates. Place a small nonreactive saucepan over medium heat. Add the cooking oil and ginger. When the ginger begins to sizzle but has not browned, add the balsamic essence. Bring to a boil. Remove from the heat, and stir in the cilantro and butter, stirring until the butter is completely melted. Spoon the sauce over the swordfish and serve at once.

In this recipe, half a pineapple is cut into long strips, rubbed with brown sugar and grilled alongside the salmon. The rest of the pineapple is puréed in a food processor, then combined with soy, ginger, and lots of chopped cilantro. Because the pineapple has a high acid content, marinate the salmon for no more than 30 minutes, or the pineapple will cause the texture of the salmon to deteriorate. Choose a perfectly ripe pineapple, which will feel slightly soft and whose outside color will have changed from a greenish-brown to a faint yellow. As a possible menu, accompany this dish with rice pilaf with pecans, avocado and goat cheese salad, and hot peach crisp.

Salmon with Pineapple Glaze

Serves 4 as an entrée

INGREDIENTS

3-pound fresh salmon fillet, skin on and pin bones removed by fish vendor

½ ripe pineapple, peeled and cored

¼ cup packed brown sugar

PINEAPPLE GLAZE

½ ripe pineapple, peeled and cored

¼ cup flavorless cooking oil

¼ cup light brown sugar

¼ cup thin soy sauce

¼ cup finely minced ginger

¼ cup minced green onion

½ cup chopped cilantro sprigs

2 serrano chiles, finely minced, including the seeds

ADVANCE PREPARATION

Keep the salmon refrigerated. Slice the pineapple into 6 long pieces. Rub with the brown sugar, and set aside. To make the pineapple glaze: finely mince the pineapple in a food processor until it is nearly liquefied. Transfer to a bowl and add all the remaining ingredients. Stir well, then refrigerate. *All advance preparation may be completed up to 8 hours before you begin the final steps.*

FINAL STEPS

Place the salmon in a nonreactive container. At least 10 minutes but not more than 30 minutes in advance of cooking, pour the glaze over the salmon. Turn the salmon over so that it is evenly coated. Keep refrigerated.

To Grill: If using a gas or electric grill, preheat to medium (350°). If using charcoal or wood, prepare a fire. When the gas or electric grill is preheated or the coals or wood are ash covered, brush the cooking rack with the oil, then lay the salmon skin-side down in the center of the grill. Cover the grill and regulate the heat so that it remains at a medium temperature. Grill the salmon for about 12 to 14 minutes, never turning it over, but basting it with the glaze every time you lift the grill lid.

To Smoke: Bring the fish to room temperature, about 15 minutes. Prepare the smoker for barbecuing, bringing the temperature to 200° to 220°. Smoke the salmon for about 45 minutes, or until it just begins to flake. During smoking, brush on more of the marinade.

To Broil: Preheat the broiler. Place the salmon 4 inches from the heat source, skin-side down, and broil for about 12 minutes, or until the salmon just loses it raw interior color and begins to flake when prodded with a fork. If the salmon begins to brown too much, turn off the broiler and bake the salmon at 500°.

To Serve: During the last 4 minutes of cooking, grill or broil the pineapple strips until they turn gold on both sides, or smoke the pineapple strips during the last 15 minutes of smoking. When the salmon just begins to flake when prodded with a knife and fork, gently slide 2 large metal spatulas under the fillet and transfer it to a heated serving platter. Serve at once, accompanied with the pineapple strips.

*T*his method of cooking salmon, first introduced to us by friends in Calgary, Ontario, is an ancient technique used by Pacific Northwest Indians. The smoky essence from the cedar plank infuses the salmon with a fantastic flavor. Usually, burning softwoods on the grill creates an unpleasant taste, but cedar is the exception! For a variation, substitute any untreated hardwood plank (available at lumberyards) cut to the size of 2 x 6 x 18 inches. Caution: Do not use treated hardwood, which is highly poisonous. Soak the plank for 1 to 24 hours. You will be able to reuse the plank eight to twelve times before it burns away completely. This technique works great for all fish fillets, and you can vary the flavor by substituting any of the other marinades or rubs in this chapter. As a possible menu, accompany this dish with homemade rolls, baby green beans, fresh tomatoes, and three-nut tart.

Planked Salmon with Ginger Spice Rub

Serves 6 to 8 as an entrée

INGREDIENTS

1 untreated cedar plank, 2 x 6 x 18 inches

3- to 4-pound fresh salmon fillet, skin on and pin bones removed by fish vendor

⅓ cup very finely minced ginger

SPICE RUB

10 tablespoons packed light brown sugar

2 to 3 teaspoons salt

1 tablespoon ground allspice

1 tablespoon ground nutmeg

1 tablespoon ground cloves

1 tablespoon ground coriander

1 tablespoon finely ground white pepper

ADVANCE PREPARATION

Soak the plank in water for 1 to 24 hours. The plank will float—that's fine! Keep the salmon refrigerated. Set aside the ginger. In a small bowl, combine the rub ingredients. Mix well. *All advance preparation may be completed up to 24 hours before you begin the final steps.*

FINAL STEPS

Just before cooking, place the salmon on the plank. Score the salmon lengthwise and crosswise, making cuts that go up to, but not through the skin, and are ½ inch apart. Rub the ginger over the salmon and into the cuts. Sprinkle on about 4 to 5 tablespoons of the rub, rubbing it over the salmon and deeply into the cuts. The unused rub can be bottled and stored on the spice rack.

To Grill: If using a gas or electric grill, preheat to medium (350°). If using charcoal or wood, prepare a fire

When the gas or electric grill is preheated or the coals or wood are ash covered, lay the plank on the barbecue. When the plank begins to smoke, cover the grill. Cook for about 17 minutes, or until the flesh of the salmon begins to flake when prodded with a knife and fork.

To serve: Gently slide 2 large metal spatulas under the fillet and transfer it to a heated serving platter. Or, transfer the cedar plank to a wooden platter lined with aluminum foil, and bring the salmon to the table on the smoking plank! Serve at once.

In Japan, teriyaki sauce is brushed on skewered pieces of meat or seafood as they are grilled. Bottled teriyaki sauces have a simple taste, but homemade teriyaki sauce can be glorious. In this recipe, a combination of sweet and dry sake, dark soy, sugar, ginger, and chopped basil is boiled until it becomes a syrup, and at the very end, several tablespoons of unsalted butter are stirred into the sauce. The taste is fantastic! Try brushing this on other types of fish or poultry as they cook on the grill. A word of warning: Don't use this sauce as a marinade because its salt content will cause the texture of the fish or poultry to deteriorate. As a possible menu, accompany this dish with green bean and almond salad, grilled red potatoes, and yellow watermelon sorbet.

Teriyaki Salmon

Serves 4 as an entrée

INGREDIENTS

4 fresh salmon steaks, each about ½ inch thick

Flavorless cooking oil to brush on the cooking rack

TERIYAKI SAUCE

¾ cup mirin (Japanese cooking rice wine)

¾ cup sake

¾ cup dark soy sauce

3 tablespoons sugar

3 tablespoons very finely minced ginger

2 tablespoons minced fresh basil leaves

2 tablespoons unsalted butter, at room temperature

ADVANCE PREPARATION

Keep the salmon refrigerated. In a small saucepan, combine the mirin, sake, soy, sugar, ginger, and basil. Bring to a boil and cook until 1 cup remains. Remove from heat, stir in the butter, then cover and set aside at room temperature. *All advance preparation may be completed up to 8 hours before you begin the final steps.*

FINAL STEPS

Place the salmon in a nonreactive container. At least 10 minutes but not more than 30 minutes in advance of cooking, pour the marinade over the salmon. Turn the salmon over so that it is evenly coated. Keep refrigerated.

To Grill: If using a gas or electric grill, preheat to medium (350°). If using charcoal or wood, prepare a fire. When the gas or electric grill is preheated or the coals or wood are ash covered, brush the cooking rack with the oil. Lay the salmon in the center of the grill. Cover the grill and regulate the heat so that it remains at a medium temperature. Grill the salmon until it just begins to flake when prodded with a fork, about 4 minutes on each side, turning the salmon once. As the salmon cooks, brush on the remaining marinade.

To Smoke: Bring the fish to room temperature, about 15 minutes. Prepare the smoker for barbecuing, bringing the temperature to 200° to 220°. Smoke the salmon for about 45 minutes, or until it just begins to flake. During smoking, brush on more of the marinade.

To Broil: Preheat the broiler. Place the salmon 4 inches from the heat source and broil for about 4 minutes on each side, or until the salmon begins to flake when prodded with a fork. If the salmon begins to brown too much, turn off the broiler and bake at 500°.

To Serve: Transfer the salmon to a heated serving platter or 4 heated dinner plates and serve at once.

The secret to grilling tuna perfectly is to sear the outside over high heat and then to remove the tuna when the interior is rare to medium rare. Because tuna is extremely lean, any further cooking creates such a dry-tasting fish that it becomes completely unpalatable. Always buy the brilliantly red, very finely grained sashimi-grade tuna rather than the less expensive, and more common, coarse-grained and lighter-colored tuna. If the tuna steaks have a darker section, called the "blood line," do not cut it out; in doing so you will disfigure the steak, and many people prefer this richer-tasting section. As a possible menu, accompany the dish with fruit salsa (see page 54), coconut steamed rice, and green tea ice cream.

Tuna with Wasabi Ginger

Serves 4 as an entrée

INGREDIENTS

2 pounds fresh tuna steaks

Flavorless cooking oil to brush on the cooking rack

1 bunch fresh chives

WASABI-GINGER RUB

½ cup freshly squeezed lemon juice

½ cup thin soy sauce

½ cup mirin (Japanese cooking rice wine)

2 tablespoons packed light brown sugar

¼ cup finely minced ginger

1½ tablespoons Japanese wasabi powder

2 tablespoons unsalted butter

ADVANCE PREPARATION

Keep the tuna refrigerated. Set aside the cooking oil and chives. Prepare the rub: In a small nonreactive saucepan, combine the lemon juice, soy sauce, mirin, brown sugar, and ginger. Bring to a boil over high heat and boil until only ½ cup remains, about 5 minutes. It will be very syrupy. Transfer to a bowl and stir in the wasabi powder and butter. Set aside. *All advance preparation may be completed up to 8 hours before you begin the final steps.*

FINAL STEPS

Place the tuna in a nonreactive container, add the wasabi marinade, and coat the pieces evenly. Marinate 15 to 30 minutes, refrigerated. Mince the chives.

To Grill: If using a gas or electric grill, preheat to high (500°). If using charcoal or wood, prepare a fire. When the gas or electric grill is preheated or the coals or wood are ash covered, brush the cooking rack with the oil. Lay the tuna in the center of the grill. Cover the grill and regulate the heat so that it remains at a high temperature. Grill the tuna for about 2 minutes on each side, brushing on more of the marinade. Remove the tuna when it is lightly browned on the outside and rare in the center.

To Broil: Preheat the broiler. Place the tuna about 4 inches from the heat source and broil for about 2 minutes on each side, or until the outside of the tuna has browned lightly but the interior is still rare.

To Serve: Transfer the tuna to a heated serving platter or 4 heated dinner plates. Sprinkle with the chives and serve at once.

There are dozens of grill models to choose from. Whether you grill on an apartment balcony or next to a swimming pool, buy the largest grill possible. The bigger the grill, the more room you will have to move food from hotter to cooler areas, and the more you can cook! The following list is just a hint of the many grills available for home cooking. For the widest selection, go to a store that specializes in grills and smokers.

Hot Grilling Equipment

Hibachis: These small, portable grills are fine for use on apartment balconies, at picnics, and for tailgate parties. Because they have no cover, hibachis are only good for grilling fish, quick-cooking meats, and vegetables. Be sure to place a hibachi on a heat-proof surface.

Covered Charcoal Grills: Covered charcoal grills can be used for grilling all types of seafood, tender cuts of meats, and vegetables, as well as for slow smoking. While it does take time to prepare the fire, the flavor is far superior to foods cooked on gas and electric grills. There are many types of covered grills, including the popular kettle grills made by Weber.

Gas Grills: Gas grills are so easy to use that they make grilling a perfect choice for weeknights. Gas grills are not as versatile as charcoal grills, because the gas heat, even at the lowest setting, is still too hot for slow-smoking. Of the dozens of different types of gas grills available, we prefer the models made by Weber. In our limited amount of product testing, we have found that the more expensive gas grills produce more heat, more evenly, and usually have a convenient attached work counter. Furthermore, the more expensive models are engineered with metal cross bars or lava rocks so that as the marinade and moisture drip from the food, they vaporize and create smoke. This gives the food additional flavor. Your fuel source can be an attached propane tank, or the grill can be hand-plumbed into your natural gas line.

Built-in Indoor Grills: Many manufacturers offer built-in or electric indoor grills as part of a stove or as a separate unit. Grilling indoors requires good ventilation. Grills that have a down-draft ventilation system are good only for grilling vegetables, seafood, boneless chicken breasts, and very thin steaks. The best built-in indoor grills, such as those made by Viking, Wolf, and Thermador, require an expensive hood system. These grills work wonderfully for cooking seafood, bone-in chicken, and thick steaks.

Portable Stove-Top Grills: Single- and double-burner portable grill pans work great on both gas and electric stove tops for cooking vegetables, seafood, boneless chicken breasts, and very thin steaks. The ridges cause the marinade on the underside of the food to vaporize, the food sears quickly, and the ridges create beautiful markings on the food. To use, place the grill on the back burner(s) so that the stove's hood system is more effective in venting the fumes. The best model is the cast-iron Le Creuset grill, which covers two burners.

Safety Precautions

- Never light briquettes or lump charcoal with gasoline.

- Never spray lighter fluid onto coals that have already been lighted. The lighter fluid container can explode.

- Never place an electric starter or metal chimney that has just been removed from the coals where it could accidentally be touched by people or animals.

- Keep all children away from the grilling area. It is not a play area.

- Never cook on a charcoal grill indoors, or use any type of grill in the garage, under any overhang, within 4 feet of a wall, or near any low overhanging trees.

- Wait 24 hours before removing coals from a grill. Hot coals placed in a garbage can or tipped onto a trash pile will start a fire.

- Always ignite gas grills with the top off.

- Always turn the gas grill off the moment the food has been removed and the grill scrubbed. Forgetting to turn the grill off is dangerous.

- Always follow the manufacturer's safety cautions when using charcoal and gas grills.

This marinade has sparkling "high notes" from the lemon zest, ginger, and Asian chile sauce, and a long lingering flavor finish from the soy and oyster sauce. Pick accompanying dishes that provide a dramatic color and textural contrast to the halibut, and that are mild in flavor so the marinade is the star. Good choices would be a wild rice dish flecked with pine nuts and parsley, cooked ahead and reheated for dinner, and thick slices of vine-ripened yellow tomatoes with a drizzle of extra-virgin olive oil, balsamic vinegar, and basil slivers. Your dinner guests will cheer even louder if you conclude the dinner with slices of flourless chocolate cake served on raspberry sauce.

Halibut in Lemon-Ginger Marinade —————— *Serves 4 as an entrée*

INGREDIENTS

2 pounds fresh halibut steaks, 1 inch
  thick
Flavorless cooking oil to brush on the
  cooking rack

LEMON-GINGER MARINADE

1 tablespoon finely minced lemon zest
⅓ cup freshly squeezed lemon juice
¼ cup dry white wine or dry vermouth
3 tablespoons flavorless cooking oil
2 tablespoons thin soy sauce
1 tablespoon oyster sauce
¼ teaspoon Asian chile sauce or freshly
  ground black pepper
¼ cup minced green onions
1 tablespoon very finely minced ginger
2 cloves garlic, finely minced

ADVANCE PREPARATION

Place the halibut in a nonreactive container and refrigerate. Set aside the cooking oil, if grilling. Combine all the marinade ingredients; if not using right away, cover and refrigerate. *All advance preparation may be completed up to 8 hours before you begin the final steps.*

FINAL STEPS

At least 10 minutes but not more than 30 minutes prior to cooking, pour the marinade over the halibut and turn it to evenly coat. Keep refrigerated.

To Grill: If using a gas or electric grill, preheat to medium (350°). If using charcoal or wood, prepare a fire. When the gas or electric grill is preheated or the coals or wood are ash covered, brush the cooking rack with the oil. Lay the steaks in the center of the grill. Cover the grill and regulate the heat so that it remains at a medium temperature. Grill the steaks until they just begin to flake when prodded with a fork, about 4 minutes on each side. As the fish cooks, brush on the remaining marinade.

To Smoke: Bring the fish to room temperature, about 15 minutes. Prepare the smoker for barbecuing, bringing the temperature to 200° to 220°. Smoke the halibut for about 45 minutes, or until it just begins to flake when prodded with a fork. During smoking, brush on more of the marinade.

To Broil: Preheat the broiler. Place the halibut 4 inches from the heat source and broil for approximately 4 minutes on each side, or until the steaks just begin to flake. If the halibut begins to brown too much, turn off the broiler and bake at 500°. During cooking, brush on more of the marinade.

To Serve: Transfer the halibut to a heated serving platter or 4 heated dinner plates and serve at once.

This marinade, which was one of the most popular marinades I developed for a restaurant on Melrose Avenue in Hollywood, is great on scallops, halibut, swordfish, poultry, and pork. Since the flavors are quite assertive, use it on seafood only as a marinade. On the other hand, when substituting meat, set aside 1/2 cup at room temperature, then after the meat has been marinated, grilled, and placed on the dinner plates, add a spoonful of the reserved marinade. This adds a burst of flavor. As a possible menu, accompany this dish with garlic-herb bread, tomato-cucumber salad, and homemade peppermint ice cream.

Thai-High Barbecued Shrimp

Serves 4 as an entrée

INGREDIENTS

2 pounds large raw shrimp (about 40)

Lime slices for garnish (optional)

THAI-HIGH MARINADE

6 cloves garlic, minced

2 tablespoons finely minced ginger

4 serrano chiles, minced, including seeds

2 whole green onions, minced

¼ cup chopped cilantro sprigs

1 tablespoon finely minced lime zest

¼ cup freshly squeezed lime juice

¼ cup hoisin sauce

¼ cup red wine vinegar

¼ cup Thai fish sauce or thin soy sauce

¼ cup honey

2 tablespoons dark soy sauce

2 tablespoons flavorless cooking oil

ADVANCE PREPARATION

Using scissors, cut the shrimp shells along the back. Cut deeply into the shrimp, then rinse away the veins. Cover and refrigerate the shrimp. In a small bowl, combine all the marinade ingredients and stir well. If not using right away, cover and refrigerate. *All advance preparation may be completed up to 8 hours before you begin the final steps.*

FINAL STEPS

Slice limes. Within 30 minutes of cooking, spoon the marinade under the shrimp shells. Keep refrigerated.

To Grill: If using a gas or electric grill, preheat to medium (350°). If using charcoal or wood, prepare a fire. When the gas or electric grill is preheated or the coals or wood are ash covered, brush the cooking rack with the oil, then lay the shrimp on the grill or on a grill screen. Grill the shrimp on both sides until they are evenly pink on the outside and white throughout, about 4 minutes' total cooking time (cut into a shrimp to check doneness). As the shrimp cooks, brush on the marinade.

To Smoke: Bring the shrimp to room temperature, about 15 minutes. Prepare the smoker for barbecuing, bringing the temperature to 200° to 220°. Smoke the shrimp for about 15 to 20 minutes, or until they are evenly pink on the outside and white throughout. During smoking, brush on more of the marinade.

To Broil: Preheat the broiler. Place the shrimp 4 inches from the heat source and broil for about 4 minutes, or until they are evenly pink on the outside and white throughout.

To Serve: Transfer the shrimp to a heated serving platter or 4 heated dinner plates, garnish with lime slices, and serve at once.

Seasoned butters are easy to make, can be stored indefinitely in the freezer, and contribute a marvelous flavor to all types of grilled seafood. In a food processor, finely mince garlic, ginger, shallots, or chiles, or any combination of these ingredients, to yield about ¹/₄ cup. Add to the food processor about 1 cup of fresh herbs and mince finely. Then add 1 cup of room temperature unsalted butter, plus any seasoning such as minced citrus zest, ground spices, or a bottled condiment. Process until evenly blended. If planning to store it for more than a few days, chill the butter, roll it into a cylinder, wrap it tightly with plastic wrap, and freeze. The next time you need to add a little flavor jolt to seafood on the grill, place slices of butter on the seafood as it finishes cooking. As a possible menu, accompany this dish with wild rice with currants, chilled asparagus salad, and fresh strawberries with chocolate sauce.

Shrimp with Herb Butter

Serves 4 as an entrée

INGREDIENTS

2 pounds large raw shrimp (about 40)

Flavorless cooking oil to brush on the cooking rack

HERB-BUTTER GLAZE

1 cup (2 sticks) unsalted butter, at room temperature

2 teaspoons Asian chile sauce

1 teaspoon ground Szechwan pepper (optional)

¾ teaspoon salt

12 cloves garlic, finely minced

2 tablespoons finely minced lime zest

½ cup freshly squeezed lime juice

2 bunches fresh chives, minced

⅔ cup chopped cilantro sprigs

ADVANCE PREPARATION

Shell the shrimp, cut them deeply lengthwise, and rinse out the vein. Pat dry, cover, and refrigerate. Set aside the cooking oil, if grilling. Place all the herb-butter glaze ingredients in a small nonreactive saucepan, cover, and refrigerate. *All advance preparation may be completed up to 8 hours before you begin the final steps.*

FINAL STEPS

Place the saucepan containing the glaze mixture over medium-low heat. Heat until the butter melts and the garlic begins to sizzle. Cool the glaze to room temperature. Place the shrimp in a bowl, add the glaze, and toss to evenly coat. Keep refrigerated.

To Grill: If using a gas or electric grill, preheat to medium (350°). If using charcoal or wood, prepare a fire. When the gas or electric grill is preheated or the coals or wood are ash covered, brush the cooking rack with the oil, and lay the shrimp on the grill or on a grill screen. Grill the shrimp on both sides until they are evenly pink on the outside and white throughout, about 4 minutes' total cooking time (cut into a shrimp to check). As the shrimp cook, brush on the remaining herb-butter glaze.

To Smoke: Bring the shrimp to room temperature, about 15 minutes. Prepare the smoker for barbecuing, bringing the temperature to 200° to 220°. Smoke the shrimp for about 15 to 20 minutes, or until they are evenly pink on the outside and white throughout. During smoking, brush on more of the herb-butter glaze.

To Broil: Preheat the broiler. Place the shrimp 4 inches from the heat source and broil for about 4 minutes, or until they are evenly pink on the outside and white throughout.

To Serve: Transfer the shrimp to a heated serving platter or 4 heated dinner plates and serve at once.

This assertive marinade should be used only as a marinade and basting sauce so that the heat of the grill tempers the intense flavors of rum, garlic, and chile. If you are not a fan of rum, substitute Grand Marnier or 1/2 cup freshly squeezed lime juice, or utilize one of the other marinades in this chapter. Strips of fresh pineapple, rubbed with a little brown sugar and grilled alongside the shrimp, would make a great addition. As a possible menu, accompany this dish with mashed yams, mango salad with baby greens, and Key lime pie.

Shrimp with Caribbean Rum Marinade

Serves 4 as an entrée

INGREDIENTS
2 pounds large raw shrimp (about 40)
Flavorless cooking oil to brush on the
    cooking rack

CARIBBEAN RUM MARINADE
1 cup rum
¼ cup butter, melted
¼ cup honey
1 tablespoon pure vanilla extract
1 teaspoon ground allspice
1 teaspoon ground cinnamon
½ cup chopped cilantro sprigs
3 tablespoons very finely minced ginger
4 cloves garlic, finely minced
1 Scotch bonnet chile, or 4 serrano chiles,
    finely minced, including the seeds
Finely minced zest from 1 lemon

ADVANCE PREPARATION
Shell the shrimp, cut the shrimp deeply lengthwise, and rinse out the vein. Pat dry, cover, and refrigerate. Set aside the cooking oil, if grilling. In a small bowl, combine all the marinade ingredients and mix well. If not using right away, cover and refrigerate. *All advance preparation may be completed up to 8 hours before you begin the final steps.*

FINAL STEPS
Place the shrimp in a bowl. At least 10 minutes but not more than 30 minutes in advance of cooking, pour the marinade over the shrimp. Toss the shrimp to coat evenly. Keep refrigerated.

To Grill: If using a gas or electric grill, preheat to medium (350°). If using charcoal or wood, prepare a fire. When the gas or electric grill is preheated or the coals or wood are ash covered, brush the cooking rack with the oil, then lay the shrimp on the grill or on a grill screen. Grill the shrimp on both sides until they are evenly pink on the outside and white throughout, about 4 minutes' total cooking time (cut into a shrimp to check). As the shrimp cook, brush on the remaining marinade.

To Smoke: Bring the shrimp to room temperature. Prepare the smoker for barbecuing, bringing the temperature to 200° to 220°. Smoke the shrimp for about 15 to 20 minutes, or until they are evenly pink on the outside and white throughout. During smoking, brush on more of the marinade.

To Broil: Preheat the broiler. Place the shrimp 4 inches from the heat source and broil for about 2 minutes on each side, or until they are evenly pink on the outside and white throughout.

To Serve: Transfer the shrimp to a heated serving platter or 4 heated dinner plates and serve at once.

G reen curry paste is the very spicy Thai equivalent to Italian pesto. They both rely on fresh herbs and seasonings that are finely puréed then made into a paste by the addition of oil. While both can be stored in the refrigerator for several days or frozen, their intense fresh herb flavor is at its peak when used the day they are made. In the following recipe, you can reduce the amount of fresh chiles, or add mint and chives to the herb blend. As a possible menu, accompany this dish with coconut rice pilaf, green papaya salad, and bananas flambé.

Tiger Prawns with Green Curry Rub

Serves 4 as an entrée

INGREDIENTS

2 pounds large raw shrimp (about 40)

Flavorless cooking oil to brush on the cooking rack

2 limes

GREEN CURRY PASTE

4 whole cloves

12 black peppercorns

2 teaspoons coriander seeds

1 teaspoon caraway seeds

½ teaspoon cumin seeds

6 cloves garlic, peeled

1 medium-sized shallot, peeled

3 whole serrano chiles, stemmed

1½ cups mixed fresh basil leaves and cilantro sprigs

1 teaspoon salt

½ cup flavorless cooking oil

ADVANCE PREPARATION

Shell the shrimp, cut them deeply lengthwise, and rinse out the vein. Pat dry, cover, and refrigerate. Set aside the cooking oil, if grilling. Cut the limes into wedges, cover, and refrigerate. Prepare the green curry paste: Place the cloves, peppercorns, coriander, caraway, and cumin seeds in a small dry sauté pan. Place the pan over medium heat and cook until the spices just begin to smoke, about 3 minutes. In an electric spice grinder, grind the spices into a powder. In a food processor, mince the garlic, shallot, and chiles. Add the basil and cilantro and salt, then mince very finely. Add the ground spices and mince again. With the machine running, slowly pour the ½ cup cooking oil down the feed tube and mince until a paste is formed. Transfer to a small bowl, cover and refrigerate. *All advance preparation may be completed up to 8 hours before you begin the final steps.*

FINAL STEPS

Within 30 minutes of cooking, rub the shrimp with the green curry paste. Keep refrigerated.

To Grill: If using a gas or electric grill, pre-heat to medium (350°). If using charcoal or wood, prepare a fire. When the gas or electric grill is preheated or the coals or wood are ash covered, brush the cooking rack with the oil, then lay the shrimp on the grill or on a grill screen. Grill the shrimp on both sides until they are evenly pink on the outside and white throughout, about 4 minutes' total cooking time (cut into a shrimp to check on doneness).

To Smoke: Bring the shrimp to room temperature, about 15 minutes. Prepare the smoker for barbecuing, bringing the temperature to 200°. Smoke the shrimp for about 15 to 20 minutes, or until they are evenly pink on the outside and white throughout (cut into one).

To Broil: Preheat the broiler. Place the shrimp 4 inches from the heat source and broil for about 4 minutes, or until they are evenly pink on the outside and white throughout.

To Serve: Transfer the shrimp to a heated serving platter or 4 heated dinner plates and serve at once, accompanied with lime wedges.

ew things are worse than watching expensive sea scallops fall through the grill grids onto the hot coals. When grilling sea scallops, place them on a grill screen (see page 42) that has been preheated on top of the grill, or do the following: Run 2 skewers through a scallop, then thread additional scallops on the doubled skewers until they are nearly filled. Now the scallops will be easy to turn over, none of them will spin on the skewer, and they will never fall through the grids. As a possible menu, accompany this dish with watercress-tomato pasta salad and pecan praline pie.

Sea Scallops Brushed with Cajun Butter

Serves 4 as an entrée

INGREDIENTS

2 pounds large fresh sea scallops

Flavorless cooking oil to brush on the
    cooking rack

2 lemons

CAJUN BUTTER

8 cloves garlic, peeled

2 shallots, peeled

¼ cup chopped fresh basil leaves

1 tablespoon fresh thyme leaves

1 cup (2 sticks) unsalted butter, at room
    temperature

1 tablespoon Worcestershire sauce

½ teaspoon salt

½ teaspoon freshly ground black pepper

½ teaspoon freshly ground white pepper

¼ teaspoon cayenne pepper

ADVANCE PREPARATION

Pull off and discard the little secondary muscle lying along one side of each scallop. Place the scallops in a bowl, cover, and refrigerate. Set aside the cooking oil, if grilling. Cut the lemons into wedges, cover, and refrigerate. Make the Cajun butter: In a food processor, mince the garlic and shallots. Add the basil and thyme, then mince. Add the remaining ingredients and process until smooth. Transfer to a small bowl, cover and refrigerate. *All advance preparation may be completed up to 8 hours before you begin the final steps.*

FINAL STEPS

Within 5 minutes of cooking, transfer the Cajun butter to a small saucepan and melt over low heat.

To Grill: If using a gas or electric grill, preheat to medium (350°). If using charcoal or wood, prepare a fire. When the gas or electric grill is preheated or the coals or wood are ash covered, brush the cooking rack with the oil, then lay the scallops on the grill or on a grill screen. Grill the scallops on both sides just until they become firm to the touch and are opaque throughout, about 5 minutes' total cooking time (cut into one). As the scallops cook, brush on the Cajun butter.

To Smoke: Bring the scallops to room temperature, about 15 minutes. Prepare the smoker for barbecuing, bringing the temperature to 200° to 220°. Smoke the scallops for about 15 to 20 minutes, or until they are firm to the touch and opaque throughout. During smoking, brush on more of the Cajun butter.

To Broil: Preheat the broiler. Place the scallops 4 inches from the heat source and broil for about 4 minutes, or until they are firm to the touch and opaque throughout. Brush with the Cajun butter.

To Serve: Transfer the scallops to a heated serving platter or 4 heated dinner plates and serve at once, accompanied with the lemon wedges.

Sizzling and Smoking Poultry

ew aromas can rival those of chicken, game hens, and other birds sizzling on the grill. Grilling and smoking are the easiest ways to create complex-tasting poultry dishes with a minimum of preparation and only occasional supervision during cooking. Grilling sears and traps the juices, browns and crisps the skin, and concentrates and caramelizes the marinade, infusing the flesh with unique smoky essences. Smoking slow-cooks birds so that the flesh captures all of the smoky essences, the marinade permeates to the bone, and the meat achieves an unrivaled tenderness.

Chicken: Grilling and smoking will transform even an ordinary supermarket chicken into an exciting taste triumph. Cook whole or halved chicken until the thigh meat registers 170° or the juice runs clear when a thigh is prodded deeply with a fork. Cook bone-in chicken breasts to a temperature of 160°, and boneless chicken breasts with or without skin, to an internal temperature of 155° (cut into the chicken: the meat will just have lost all its pink coloring).

Game Hens: Grill and smoke game hens that have been split in half. Cook them until the internal temperature reaches 160°.

Duck, Squab, and Quail: Split duck in half or cut into pieces. Trim off all excess fat from the edges of the pieces. Score the skin. If grilling, grill over indirect heat. If smoking, brown duck, skin-side down, in a heavy frying pan to render the skin. When the skin becomes golden, transfer the duck to the smoker and cook the pieces for about 2 hours. Grill or smoke squab and quail whole or split in half. Cook squab until the internal temperature reaches 145° to 150° and the meat is still pink in the center, about 15 to 20 minutes on the grill. Grill quail for about 10 minutes. Smoked squab will be cooked in about 1½ hours and quail in about 1 hour.

Points to Remember when Grilling and Smoking Chicken and Game Hens

- All grilled and smoked chicken will taste best if you use organically raised or kosher chicken rather than the mass-produced chicken sold wrapped in plastic by most supermarkets.

- The texture and flavor of chicken and game hens improves by being soaked in a brine mixture for 4 hours, covered and refrigerated. Then remove from the brine, rinse with cold water, pat dry, and marinate. To learn about brining, see page 89.

- Marinate poultry for at least 15 minutes or up to 8 hours, covered and refrigerated.

- If chicken or game hens have been split in half, slide your finger underneath the skin along the top of the breast, loosen the chicken skin, add about ¼ cup marinade, and work this underneath the skin and across the entire surface of the breast and leg meat. Rub extra marinade across the outside of the bird, then refrigerate.

- To prevent possible bacterial contamination, never brush any marinade over the bird during the last 5 minutes of grilling. You can reserve a little of the marinade *prior* to marinating, then spoon this over the pieces once they have been cooked and transferred to dinner plates.

- Always grill chicken and game hens over medium heat.

- Since dark meat takes longer to grill, add thighs and drumsticks 8 to 10 minutes before adding breasts; or, when the breasts are almost cooked, move them to the outside edges of the grill, which are cooler.

- If the marinade has more than ¼ cup sugar or honey, grill chicken and game hens by the indirect method (see page 11), with a drip pan underneath the birds.

- The only way to cook whole chicken is by the indirect method (see "Hot Grilling Techniques," page 11).

- Grill chicken and game hens skin-side up for the first 5 to 8 minutes of cooking, then turn the pieces over every 5 minutes, brushing on more marinade and grilling until done.

- If you want less smoky flavor when smoking poultry, remove the meat from the smoker about halfway through the smoking process and finish cooking it on the grill.

There are many possible variations for this recipe. Substitute another orange liquor or replace it with freshly squeezed orange juice or fresh pineapple puréed in a blender or food processor. Add 4 minced garlic cloves; use cilantro or mint instead of basil; or substitute several minced serrano chiles for the chile sauce. If you want a richer flavor, use oyster sauce in place of the soy. While the chicken tastes fine when marinated for just 30 minutes, the flavors are much more pronounced when it is marinated for 8 hours. As a possible menu, accompany this dish with hot flour tortillas, salsa, papaya and avocado salad, and fudge ice cream.

Chicken Grand Marnier

Serves 4 as an entrée

INGREDIENTS

2 frying chickens, cut into pieces

Flavorless cooking oil to brush on the cooking rack

GRAND MARNIER MARINADE

6 tablespoons Grand Marnier

¼ cup freshly squeezed lime juice

¼ cup thin soy sauce

3 tablespoons honey

2 teaspoons Asian chile sauce

1 teaspoon salt

1 tablespoon finely minced orange zest

¼ cup very finely minced ginger

¼ cup chopped fresh basil

2 whole green onions, minced

ADVANCE PREPARATION

Rinse the chicken, pat dry, and place in a bowl. Set aside the cooking oil, if grilling. Combine the marinade ingredients and mix well. Add half the marinade to the chicken and coat the pieces evenly. Cover and refrigerate for at least 30 minutes or up to 8 hours. Reserve the other half of the marinade, which will become the Grand Marnier sauce. *All advance preparation may be completed up to 8 hours before you begin the final steps.*

FINAL STEPS

Just prior to cooking, remove the chicken from the refrigerator.

To Grill: If using a gas or electric grill, preheat to medium (350°). If using charcoal or wood, prepare a fire. When the gas or electric grill is preheated or the coals or wood are ash covered, brush the cooking rack with the oil, then lay the chicken skin-side up in the center of the grill. Cover the grill and regulate the heat so that it remains at a medium temperature. Grill the chicken for about 12 minutes on each side. The chicken is done when the breasts register 160° and the thighs register 170° on a meat thermometer (the juices will run clear when the chicken is prodded deeply with a fork). As the chicken cooks, brush on the remaining marinade.

To Smoke: Bring the chicken to room temperature, about 30 minutes. Prepare the smoker for barbecuing, bringing the temperature to 200° to 220°. Transfer the chickens to the smoker and cook for about 1 ½ hours. The chicken is done when the juices run clear when the meat is prodded deeply with a fork. During smoking, brush on more of the marinade.

To Roast: Preheat the oven to 425°. Roast the chicken until the juices run clear when the meat is prodded deeply with a fork, about 30 minutes. Brush with the glaze as the chicken cooks.

To Serve: Transfer the chickens to a heated serving platter or 4 heated dinner plates. Spoon on the Grand Marnier sauce and serve at once.

This recipe was contributed by Tom Lambing, chef/owner of Times Change in Jackson, Mississippi. The best seats in the restaurant are along the bar, where customers can enjoy their dinner while watching Tom create his wonderfully eclectic food. The Mississippi glaze is a Southern sweet-spicy-jelly "mop" used for brushing meats that are being grilled or slow-smoked. To make the glaze, Tom uses mayhaw jelly, made from a wild berry that grows in the bayous of the Mississippi River. If it's not available in your local gourmet store, plum or red currant jelly makes a good substitute. As a possible menu, accompany this dish with corn muffins, green beans with almonds, and pineapple upside-down cake.

Mississippi Chicken

Serves 4 as an entrée

INGREDIENTS

2 frying chickens, cut into pieces
Flavorless cooking oil to brush on the
    cooking rack
Salt

MISSISSIPPI GLAZE

8 ounce jar mayhaw or plum or red
    currant jelly
¼ cup distilled white vinegar
2 tablespoons Creole or Dijon mustard
2 tablespoons prepared horseradish
1 to 2 tablespoons green Tabasco
    sauce
¼ cup chopped fresh mint leaves

ADVANCE PREPARATION

Rinse the chicken pieces, pat dry, cover, and refrigerate. Set aside the cooking oil. Make the glaze: Place the jelly in a small saucepan and melt over low heat, then stir in the vinegar, mustard, horseradish, Tabasco, and mint. Keep at room temperature. *All advance preparation may be completed up to 8 hours before you begin the final steps.*

FINAL STEPS

Just prior to cooking, remove the chicken from the refrigerator and sprinkle it with salt. Heat the glaze until it becomes a liquid.

To Grill: If using a gas or electric grill, preheat to medium (350°). If using charcoal or wood, prepare a fire. When the gas or electric grill is preheated or the coals or wood are ash covered, brush the cooking rack with the oil, then lay the chicken skin-side up in the center of the rack. Cover the grill and regulate the heat so that it remains at a medium temperature. Grill the chicken for about 12 minutes on each side. The chicken is done when the breasts register 160° and thighs register 170° on a meat thermometer (the juices will run clear when the chicken is prodded deeply with a fork). As the chicken cooks, brush on the glaze.

To Smoke: Bring the chicken to room temperature, about 30 minutes. Prepare the smoker for barbecuing, bringing the temperature to 200° to 220°. Transfer the chickens to the smoker and cook for about 1½ hours. Brush the chicken several times with the glaze. The chicken is done when the juices run clear when the meat is prodded deeply with a fork.

To Roast: Preheat the oven to 425°. Roast the chicken until the juices run clear when the meat is prodded deeply with a fork, about 30 minutes. Brush with the glaze as the chicken cooks.

To Serve: Transfer the chicken to a heated serving platter or 4 heated dinner plates.

*C*ooking chicken with the skin on gives the meat more flavor and helps prevent it from becoming dry during grilling. Since studies show that the fat content of cooked chicken meat is identical whether it has been cooked with the skin on or off, always grill the chicken skin on and let your dinner guests decide whether to remove the crispy exterior shell. Boned chicken breasts will cook in about 8 minutes, or you can substitute bone-in breasts (about 15 minutes cooking time), or whole frying chickens cut into pieces, which will take about 25 minutes to grill. As a possible menu, accompany this dish with homemade sesame rolls, watercress salad, and hot apple pie.

Chicken Breasts Caribbean

Serves 4 as an entrée

INGREDIENTS

8 chicken breast halves, boned but skin on

1/3 cup cilantro sprigs for garnish

Flavorless cooking oil to brush on the cooking rack

CARIBBEAN MARINADE

2 teaspoons finely minced orange zest

1/4 cup freshly squeezed orange or tangerine juice

1/4 cup mild olive oil

1/4 cup Grand Marnier

1/4 cup packed light brown sugar

1/4 cup thin soy sauce

2 teaspoons Asian chile sauce

1 teaspoon freshly grated nutmeg

1/2 teaspoon ground allspice

1/2 teaspoon ground cinnamon

1/4 teaspoon salt

1/4 cup chopped fresh mint leaves

2 tablespoons finely minced ginger

ADVANCE PREPARATION

Rinse the chicken pieces, pat dry, and place in a bowl. Set aside the cilantro. Set aside the cooking oil, if grilling. Combine the marinade ingredients and mix well. Add the marinade to the chicken and coat the pieces evenly. Cover and refrigerate for at least 30 minutes or up to 8 hours. *All advance preparation may be completed up to 8 hours before you begin the final steps.*

FINAL STEPS

Just prior to cooking, remove the chicken from the refrigerator.

To Grill: If using a gas or electric grill, preheat to medium (350°). If using charcoal or wood, prepare a fire. When the gas or electric grill is preheated or the coals or wood are ash covered, brush the cooking rack with the oil, then lay the chicken skin-side down in the center of the rack. Regulate the heat so that it remains at a medium temperature. Grill the chicken for about 3 to 4 minutes on each side. The chicken is done when it just loses its pink color in the center (cut into a piece). As the chicken cooks, brush on all the remaining marinade.

To Smoke: Bring the chicken to room temperature, about 30 minutes. Prepare the smoker for barbecuing, bringing the temperature to 200° to 220°. Transfer the chickens to the smoker and cook for about 30 minutes. The chicken is done when the breasts feel firm and the meat just loses its pink color in the center. During smoking, brush with the marinade.

To Broil: Preheat the broiler. Place the chicken, skin-side up, 4 inches from the heat source and broil until the skin becomes golden, about 3 minutes. Turn the chicken over, brush with the marinade, and continue broiling until the chicken just loses its pink color in the center, about another 2 minutes.

To Serve: Transfer the chicken to a heated serving platter or 4 heated dinner plates, garnish with cilantro, and serve.

Other Barbecue Equipment

Grill Screens: These fine-meshed screens are placed on the cooking rack to prevent small food such as shrimp and scallops from falling into the fire. To ease cleanup chores, purchase a nonstick grill screen, and always spray it on both sides with nonstick cooking spray prior to grilling.

Grill Baskets: These allow you to turn fragile fish without it falling apart and to hold shrimp, scallops, and vegetables. A word of warning: Buy a grill basket with a retractable handle. Otherwise, the handle will extend over the edge of the grill and make it impossible to tightly cover the grill. Always rub the grill basket with oil before adding the food.

Rib Racks, Racks for Chicken, Corn Racks, and Potato Racks: All these accessories, which are available at barbecue stores and many hardware stores, make it easier to grill or smoke a large amount of food, and to cook food more evenly.

Skewers: Metal skewers do not burn away but they are notorious for burning hands and lips. If you use bamboo skewers, soak them in cold water for 8 to 24 hours so they are less likely to become scorched. Their pliability makes it easy to thread food onto them, and they will never burn your hands. To prevent the ends of bamboo skewers from burning during grilling, place a double layer of aluminum foil under the exposed ends of the skewers.

Offset Spatulas: We prefer the large chef's spatulas sold at cookware shops and restaurant supply stores rather than the flimsy spatulas found in supermarkets. Large stainless steel spatulas, with an elevated wooden or thermoplastic handle, make it easy to transfer food to and from the grill, and to turn ingredients over.

Spring-Loaded Tongs: Settle for nothing but the best: Buy the type of tongs used by restaurant chefs and pictured here. The ends of the tongs are perfect for cradling a sauce to spoon over the food, and the spring-loaded handle makes it easy to quickly grasp ingredients. Buy tongs of varying lengths. You will want to use longer tongs when cooking over high heat or when reaching across the grill. And it is a good idea to reserve one pair of tongs just for rearranging coals or adding more coals to the fire.

Long-Handled Barbecue Forks: We never use barbecue forks because moisture escapes when the food has been pierced by the tines. Use tongs instead.

Mitts: Grills can produce a fearsome heat. Protect your hands by using heat-proof mitts such as neoprene gloves—not the little hot pads prevalent in most home kitchens. Many cooks like to move food around using a long-sleeved grill mitt reserved just for that purpose.

Basting Brushes: Inexpensive basting brushes of various sizes are available at hardware and paint stores. Use the ones made with natural bristles rather than nylon ones. Wash in soapy water rather than in the dishwasher because very hot water will loosen the bristles.

Instant-Read Meat Thermometers: Small pocket-sized instant-read meat thermometers are sold by most hardware and department stores. To use, insert the thermometer into the thickest part of the meat; in 15 seconds the dial will indicate the internal temperature. These meat thermometers, however, can be inaccurate. We recommend the new, accurate, and much faster "instant-read" electronic meat thermometer probes. Look for these at your local gourmet

shop. Regardless of which type of thermometer you use, once the thermometer registers the internal temperature, remove it from the grill, smoker, or oven. Otherwise, the thermometer will break because of the high heat.

Water Spritzers: Heavy plastic spray bottles, available at hardware stores, are a practical device for spraying coals with water when flare-ups occur.

Grill Table: If your grill or smoker does not include a built-in side counter to hold marinades, precooked and finished foods, condiments, and other accessories, improvise by setting up a flat work surface next to the grill or smoker. If purchasing a table to use for this purpose, the larger the size, the more useful you will find it. We like tables that have a shelf underneath to hold miscellaneous equipment.

Apron: If you are not sure why you need to wear an apron that extends to your knees, you'll know the reason once you begin to grill or slow-smoke.

I created this marinade for a restaurant that I helped open on Sunset Boulevard in Hollywood in 1982. The chicken quickly became one of the best-selling dishes. If you omit the green onions and cilantro, the marinade can be made in larger amounts and refrigerated indefinitely. Just add a little green onion and cilantro to the portion that you use that day. The marinade is also excellent used for spareribs and firm-fleshed fish such as mahimahi. As a possible menu, accompany this dish with fried rice, asparagus salad, and ginger ice cream.

Spicy Szechwan Chicken

excellent

— Serves 4 as an entrée

INGREDIENTS

2 frying chickens, cut into pieces

Flavorless cooking oil to brush on the cooking rack

SPICY SZECHWAN MARINADE

3 tablespoons Chinese rice wine or dry sherry

3 tablespoons hoisin sauce

3 tablespoons thin soy sauce

2 tablespoons oyster sauce

2 tablespoons red wine vinegar

1 tablespoon dark sesame oil

1 tablespoon Asian chile sauce

2 tablespoons sugar

1 tablespoon finely minced garlic

1 tablespoon very finely minced ginger

2 whole green onions, minced

¼ cup chopped cilantro sprigs

ADVANCE PREPARATION

Rinse the chicken pieces, pat dry, and place in a bowl. Set aside the cooking oil, if grilling. Combine the marinade ingredients and mix well. Add the marinade to the chicken and coat the pieces evenly. Cover and refrigerate for at least 30 minutes or up to 8 hours. *All advance preparation may be completed up to 8 hours before you begin the final steps.*

FINAL STEPS

Just prior to cooking, remove the chicken from the refrigerator.

To Grill: If using a gas or electric grill, preheat to medium (350°). If using charcoal or wood, prepare a fire. When the gas or electric grill is preheated or the coals or wood are ash covered, brush the cooking rack with the oil, then lay the chicken skin-side up in the center of the rack. Cover the grill and regulate the heat so that it remains at a medium temperature. Grill the chicken for about 12 minutes on each side. The chicken is done when the breasts register 160° and the thighs register 170° on a meat thermometer. As the chicken cooks, brush on the remaining marinade.

To Smoke: Bring the chicken to room temperature, about 30 minutes. Prepare the smoker for barbecuing, bringing the temperature to 200° to 220°. Transfer the chickens to the smoker and cook for about 1 ½ hours. The chicken is done when the juices run clear when the meat is prodded deeply with a fork. During smoking, brush with the marinade.

To Roast: Preheat the oven to 425°. Roast the chicken until the juices run clear when the meat is prodded deeply with a fork, about 30 minutes. During roasting, brush with the marinade.

To Serve: Transfer the chicken to a heated serving platter or 4 heated

For this recipe, chicken is rubbed with various dried herbs and spices, grilled, then topped with a Cajun sauce bursting with the flavors of grilled tomatoes, garlic, fresh herbs, and chiles. We have used the sauce in many other ways, such as spooning it over salmon that has been grilled, tossing 4 cups of cooked pasta with it, adding it to panfried dumplings during the final seconds of cooking, or glazing thick slices of veal meat loaf with it. As a possible menu, accompany Cajun chicken with garlic mashed potatoes, baby green beans with almonds, and chocolate bread pudding.

Cajun Chicken — *excellent* — *Serves 4 as an entrée*

INGREDIENTS

8 chicken breasts, boned but skin-on

1 bunch fresh chives

Flavorless cooking oil to brush on the
    cooking rack

CAJUN DRY RUB

2 tablespoons chile powder

1 tablespoon dried oregano

1 tablespoon dried thyme

1 tablespoon ground black pepper

1 tablespoon packed brown sugar

CAJUN HERB SAUCE

1 tablespoon unsalted butter, at room
    temperature

3 cloves garlic, finely minced

3 vine-ripened tomatoes

½ cup whipping cream

¼ cup dry vermouth

2 tablespoons oyster sauce

2 tablespoons Louisiana hot sauce or
    your favorite chile sauce

1 teaspoon sugar

2 tablespoons chopped fresh oregano
    leaves

1 tablespoon chopped fresh thyme
    leaves

ADVANCE PREPARATION

Rinse the chicken, pat dry, cover, and refrigerate. Chop the chives and set aside. Set aside the oil if grilling.

Combine all the dry rub ingredients. Rub the chicken with the dry rub on both sides, cover, and refrigerate for at least 30 minutes or up to 8 hours. Combine the butter and garlic, cover and refrigerate. Cut each tomato into 3 equal slices; place 4 inches below the heat source of a preheated broiler and broil until brown on both sides, or grill the tomatoes. Chop the tomatoes. In a small bowl, combine the tomatoes with the remaining sauce ingredients and refrigerate. *All advance preparation may be completed up to 8 hours before you begin the final steps.*

FINAL STEPS

Just prior to cooking, remove the chicken from the refrigerator.

To Grill: If using a gas or electric grill, preheat to medium (350°). If using charcoal or wood, prepare a fire. When the gas or electric grill is preheated or the coals or wood are ash covered, brush the cooking rack with the oil, then lay the chicken, skin-side down, in the center of the rack. Regulate the heat so that it remains at a medium tempera-

ture. Grill the chicken for about 3 to 4 minutes on each side. The chicken is done when it just loses its pink interior color (cut into a piece).

To Smoke: Bring chicken to room temperature, about 30 minutes. Prepare the smoker for barbecuing, bringing the temperature to 200° to 220°. Transfer the chickens to the smoker and cook for about 30 minutes. The chicken is done when the breasts feel firm and the meat just loses its pink interior color.

To Broil: Preheat the broiler. Place the chicken, skin-side up, 4 inches from the heat source, and broil until the skin becomes golden, about 3 minutes. Turn the chicken over, brush with the marinade, and continue broiling until the chicken just loses its pink interior color, about another 2 minutes.

To Serve: When the chicken is nearly done, place a small sauté pan over medium-high heat. Add the butter and garlic. When the garlic begins to sizzle, add the remaining sauce ingredients. Bring to a rapid boil and cook until it thickens enough to lightly coat a spoon, about 3 minutes. Transfer the chicken to a heated serving platter or 4 heated dinner plates. Spoon the sauce over the chicken, sprinkle with the chives, and serve at once.

The blast of flavor in this dish is derived from chipotle chiles. These smoked jalapeño chiles, simmered in a spicy tomato sauce, are sold in 4-ounce cans that are usually labeled "Chipotle Chiles in Adobo Sauce." The chipotle honey barbecue sauce can be made in larger quantities and will last indefinitely if refrigerated. It's great brushed across ribs, pork loin, butterflied leg of lamb, and rib eye steaks being readied for the grill. This recipe was contributed by executive chef Ray Breeman of the Cadillac Cafe in Denver. As a possible menu, accompany this dish with hot corn tortillas, Caesar salad, and mango sorbet.

Chicken with Chipotle Honey Barbecue Sauce

Serves 4 as an entrée

INGREDIENTS

2 frying chickens, cut into pieces

Flavorless cooking oil to brush on the cooking rack

CHIPOTLE HONEY BARBECUE SAUCE

10 cloves garlic, skin on

1 tablespoon olive oil

1¼ pounds vine-ripened tomatoes (about 4)

¼ cup minced fresh oregano

¼ cup chipotle chiles in Adobo sauce

¼ cup honey

⅓ cup molasses

⅓ cup cider vinegar

2 tablespoons dark sesame oil

1 tablespoon ground cumin

1 tablespoon kosher salt

ADVANCE PREPARATION

Rinse the chicken, pat dry, and place in a bowl. Set aside the cooking oil, if grilling.

Prepare the sauce: Rub the garlic cloves with the oil, and place the cloves on a square of aluminum foil and wrap tightly. Place in a preheated 450° oven and roast for 30 minutes, then squeeze the garlic from its peel. Place the tomatoes 4 inches from the heat source of a preheated broiler and char until the skin turns dark brown on all sides, or grill the tomatoes until the outsides are charred. Cut the tomatoes in half and seed. Place the chipotle chiles and their liquid in a blender or food processor. Purée until smooth, then add the garlic and tomato; purée. Add all the remaining ingredients and purée. Pour half of this sauce over the chicken, coat evenly, cover, and refrigerate for at least 30 minutes or up to 8 hours. Reserve the rest of the sauce in a small saucepan. *All advance preparation may be completed up to 8 hours before you begin the final steps.*

FINAL STEPS

Just prior to cooking, remove the chicken from the refrigerator.

To Grill: If using a gas or electric grill, preheat to medium (350°). If using charcoal or wood, prepare a fire. When the gas or electric grill is preheated or the coals or wood are ash covered, brush the cooking rack with the oil, then lay the chicken skin-side up in the center of the rack. Cover the grill and regulate the heat so that it remains at a medium temperature. Grill the chicken for about 12 minutes on each side. The chicken is done when the breasts register 160° and the thighs register 170° on a meat thermometer (the juices will run clear when the chicken is prodded deeply with a fork). As the chicken cooks, brush on the remaining sauce used to marinate the chicken.

To Smoke: Smoke the chicken as described on page 44. During smoking, brush with the remaining sauce used to marinate the chicken.

To Roast: Preheat the oven to 425°. Roast the chicken until the juices run clear when the meat is prodded deeply with a fork, about 30 minutes. During roasting, brush with the remaining sauce used to marinate the chicken.

To Serve: Bring the chipotle honey barbecue sauce to a boil and cook until it brightens and thickens, about 5 minutes. Transfer the chicken to a heated serving platter or 4 heated dinner plates and serve accompanied with the reserved sauce.

A long nearly every street in Thailand, roadside cooks grill chicken over charcoal on small elevated rectangular grills. Brushed with a sugar syrup infused with dried red chiles, garlic, and vinegar, Thai chicken is one of the great taste sensations. The following marinade deviates from tradition by using lime juice and lots of minced fresh herbs, but the final result is a wonderfully flavored chicken that will have your guests asking for more! Make the marinade the day you plan to use it, or the fresh taste of the herbs and lime juice will deteriorate. As a possible menu, accompany this dish with honey butter cornbread, homemade coleslaw, and peach cobbler.

Thai Barbecued Chicken

Serves 4 as an entrée

INGREDIENTS

2 frying chickens, cut into pieces

10 cilantro sprigs for garnish

Flavorless cooking oil to brush on the cooking rack

THAI BARBECUE MARINADE

6 tablespoons freshly squeezed lime juice

¼ cup freshly squeezed orange juice

¼ cup packed light brown sugar

¼ cup Thai fish sauce or thin soy sauce

¼ cup flavorless cooking oil

1 tablespoon Asian chile sauce

2 tablespoons finely minced ginger

6 cloves garlic, finely minced

¼ cup finely minced whole green onions

¼ cup minced fresh mint leaves

¼ cup minced fresh basil leaves

¼ cup minced cilantro sprigs

ADVANCE PREPARATION

Rinse the chicken pieces, pat dry, and place in a bowl. Set aside the cilantro sprigs. Set aside the cooking oil, if grilling. Combine the marinade ingredients and mix well. Add the marinade to the chicken and coat the pieces evenly. Cover and refrigerate for at least 30 minutes or up to 8 hours. *All advance preparation may be completed up to 8 hours before you begin the final steps.*

FINAL STEPS

Just prior to cooking, remove the chicken from the refrigerator.

To Grill: If using a gas or electric grill, preheat to medium (350°). If using charcoal or wood, prepare a fire. When the gas or electric grill is preheated or the coals or wood are ash covered, brush the cooking rack with the oil, then lay the chicken skin-side up in the center of the rack. Cover the grill and regulate the heat so that it remains at a medium temperature. Grill the chicken for about 12 minutes on each side. The chicken is done when the breasts register 160° and the thighs register 170° on a meat thermometer (the juices will run clear when the chicken is prodded deeply with a fork). As the chicken cooks, brush with the remaining marinade.

To Smoke: Bring the chicken to room temperature, about 30 minutes. Prepare the smoker for barbecuing, bringing the temperature to 200° to 220°. Transfer the chicken to the smoker and cook for about 1 ½ hours, or until the juices run clear when the meat is prodded deeply with a fork. During smoking, brush with the marinade.

To Roast: Preheat the oven to 425°. Roast the chicken until the juices run clear when the meat is prodded deeply with a fork, about 30 minutes. During roasting, brush with the marinade.

To Serve: Transfer the chicken to a heated serving platter or 4 heated dinner plates. Garnish with the cilantro sprigs and serve at once.

This easy-to-make marinade has a deep flavor and a wonderful versatility. The low flavor notes of hoisin sauce, red wine, and Dijon mustard provide the perfect foundation for accenting the high flavor notes of chiles, rosemary, and lemon juice. The thick marinade forms a protective shield and is great for all grilled or smoked poultry, pork, veal, and lamb. As a possible menu, accompany this dish with roasted red potatoes, avocado salad, and coconut crème brûlée.

Chicken with Rosemary, Chiles, and Hoisin

Serves 4 as an entrée

INGREDIENTS

2 frying chickens, cut into pieces

Flavorless cooking oil to brush on the
    cooking rack

ROSEMARY HOISIN MARINADE

½ cup hoisin sauce

½ cup plum sauce

½ cup dry red wine

¼ cup Dijon mustard

¼ cup freshly squeezed lemon juice

6 cloves garlic, finely minced

4 serrano chiles, finely minced,
    including seeds

¼ cup fresh rosemary sprigs, chopped

¼ cup chopped fresh sage leaves

ADVANCE PREPARATION

Rinse the chicken pieces, pat dry, and place in a bowl. Set aside the cooking oil, if grilling. Combine the marinade ingredients and mix well. Add the marinade to the chicken and coat the pieces evenly. Cover and refrigerate for at least 30 minutes or up to 8 hours. *All advance preparation may be completed up to 8 hours before you begin the final steps.*

FINAL STEPS

Just prior to cooking, remove the chicken from the refrigerator.

To Grill: If using a gas or electric grill, preheat to medium (350°). If using charcoal or wood, prepare a fire. When the gas or electric grill is preheated or the coals or wood are ash covered, brush the cooking rack with the oil, then lay the chicken, skin-side up, in the center of the rack. Cover the grill and regulate the heat so that it remains at a medium temperature. Grill the chicken for about 12 minutes on each side. The chicken is done when the breasts register 160° and the thighs register 170° on a meat thermometer (the juices will run clear when the chicken is prodded deeply with a fork). As the chicken cooks, brush on the remaining marinade.

To Smoke: Bring the chicken to room temperature, about 30 minutes. Prepare the smoker for barbecuing, bringing the temperature to 200° to 220°. Transfer the chicken to the smoker and cook for about 1 ½ hours. The chicken is done when the juices run clear when the meat is prodded deeply with a fork. During smoking, brush with the marinade.

To Roast: Preheat the oven to 425°. Roast the chicken until the juices run clear when the meat is prodded deeply with a fork, about 30 minutes. During roasting, brush with the marinade.

To Serve: Transfer the chicken to a heated serving platter or 4 heated dinner plates and serve at once.

*T*oo often barbecue cooks race between the grill and kitchen in an attempt to complete several last-minute dishes at the same time. No one enjoys this type of gastronomic kung-fu event! As a possible menu, try serving chicken Morocco with a couscous made ahead and reheated on the stovetop or in the microwave oven. Follow this course with a cucumber-yogurt salad made hours ahead and kept ready in the refrigerator. Then for dessert, choose a dish such as homemade lemon tart, or simply serve a premium ice cream surrounded by seasonal berries.

Chicken Morocco

Serves 4 as an entrée

INGREDIENTS

2 frying chickens, cut into pieces

Flavorless cooking oil to brush on the cooking rack

1 whole nutmeg

MOROCCAN LEMON MARINADE

2 tablespoons finely minced lemon zest

1 cup freshly squeezed lemon juice

½ cup olive oil

½ cup honey

2 teaspoons ground coriander seeds

2 teaspoons ground cumin

2 teaspoons sweet paprika

1 teaspoon crushed red pepper flakes

1 teaspoon salt

¼ cup very finely minced ginger

8 cloves garlic, finely minced

1 cup mixed chopped fresh cilantro, mint, and parsley

ADVANCE PREPARATION

Rinse the chicken pieces, pat dry, and place in a bowl. Set aside the cooking oil, if grilling. Combine the marinade ingredients and mix well. Add the marinade to the chicken and coat the pieces evenly. Cover and refrigerate for at least 30 minutes or up to 8 hours. *All advance preparation may be completed up to 8 hours before you begin the final steps.*

FINAL STEPS

Just prior to cooking, remove the chicken from the refrigerator.

To Grill: If using a gas or electric grill, preheat to medium (350°). If using charcoal or wood, prepare a fire. When the gas or electric grill is preheated or the coals or wood are ash covered, brush the cooking rack with the oil, then lay the chicken skin-side up in the center of the rack. Cover the grill and regulate the heat so that it remains at a medium temperature. Grill the chicken for about 12 minutes on each side. The chicken is done when the breasts register 160° and the thighs register 170° on a meat thermometer (the juices will run clear when the chicken is prodded deeply with a fork). As the chicken cooks, brush on the remaining marinade.

To Smoke: Bring the chicken to room temperature, about 30 minutes. Prepare the smoker for barbecuing, bringing the temperature to 200° to 220°. Transfer the chickens to the smoker and cook for about 1 ½ hours. The chicken is done when the juices run clear when the meat is prodded deeply with a fork. During smoking, brush with the marinade.

To Roast: Preheat the oven to 425°. Roast the chicken until the juices run clear when the meat is prodded deeply with a fork, about 30 minutes. During roasting, brush with the marinade.

To Serve: Transfer the chicken to a heated serving platter or 4 heated dinner plates. Using a nutmeg grater or cheese grater, grate a light dusting of fresh nutmeg over the chicken. Serve at once.

Salsas, Chutneys, and Condiments

The following salsas, chutneys, and condiments are used to add flavor accents to grilled and slow-smoked meats and seafood. Keep in mind that many of the marinades and barbecue sauces in this book have complex flavors and will not need accompanying sauces. We turn to these most often to perk up under-seasoned foods ranging from chilled shrimp to steaks just removed from the grill. Since many of the following accompaniments can be stored in the refrigerator, we utilize them as often as store-bought mustards and other seasonings.

Peanut Dipping Sauce

½ cup peanut butter, salted
¼ cup freshly squeezed orange juice
¼ cup Chinese rice wine or dry sherry
1 tablespoon dark soy sauce
2 tablespoons white wine vinegar
2 tablespoons honey
2 tablespoons flavorless cooking oil
1 tablespoon dark soy sauce
1 tablespoon dark sesame oil
1 tablespoon Asian chile sauce
2 cloves garlic, finely minced
2 tablespoons finely minced ginger
¼ cup minced green onion
¼ cup minced cilantro sprigs

PREPARATION
In a small bowl, combine all ingredients and mix thoroughly. Refrigerate up to 1 week. Bring to room temperature before using.

Spicy Guacamole

4 ripe avocados, peeled and pitted
½ cup chopped jicama
Kernels from 1 ear white corn
1 vine-ripened tomato, seeded and chopped
2 whole green onions, minced
¼ cup chopped cilantro sprigs
1 clove garlic, finely minced
3 tablespoons freshly squeezed lemon juice
2 teaspoons of your favorite chile sauce
½ teaspoon salt

PREPARATION
Place the avocado flesh in a bowl. Using the tines of a fork, mash the avocado into a coarse pulp with little fragments of avocado remaining. Add all the remaining ingredients and mix well. Taste and adjust the seasoning. Using a spatula, press the guacamole firmly so there are no air pockets. Sprinkle the top with a little lemon juice or cover the guacamole with a thin film of milk (not the "lactose free" variety). Press plastic wrap onto the surface and refrigerate. When ready to use, stir the guacamole, then taste and adjust the seasoning. Must be used that day. Great for most grilled and smoked shellfish and meats.

Asian Salsa

1½ pounds vine-ripened tomatoes
    (about 4 to 5 tomatoes)
3 whole green onions, minced
½ cup chopped cilantro sprigs
2 tablespoons very finely minced ginger
2 cloves garlic, finely minced
3 tablespoons red wine vinegar
2 tablespoons dark sesame oil
1 tablespoon flavorless cooking oil
1½ tablespoons sugar
2 teaspoons Asian chile sauce
½ teaspoon salt

PREPARATION
Cut the tomatoes in half crosswise. Squeeze out the seeds and mince the tomatoes. Transfer the tomatoes to a bowl, add all the remaining ingredients, and stir well. Store at room temperature. While it tastes best if used the day it is made, it can be covered and refrigerated for up to 4 days. Great for grilled and smoked seafood and meat.

Fruit Salsa

2 ripe mangoes, peeled, pitted, and finely chopped, or 2 nearly ripe papayas, peeled, seeded, and chopped, or 3 slightly firm bananas, peeled and chopped
1 ripe avocado, peeled, pitted, and cubed
1 red pepper, seeded, deribbed, and minced
¼ cup chopped cilantro sprigs
2 whole green onions, minced
2 tablespoons finely minced ginger
2 tablespoons freshly squeezed orange juice
2 tablespoons freshly squeezed lime juice
2 tablespoons packed brown sugar
1 to 2 teaspoons Asian chile sauce

PREPARATION
Within 2 hours of serving, combine all the ingredients. Taste and adjust the seasoning and keep at room temperature. You can vary the choice of fruits. This salsa is great for most grilled and smoked seafood and meats.

New Wave Tartar Sauce

1 cup mayonnaise
¼ cup minced dill pickle
2 tablespoons Grand Marnier
1 tablespoon freshly squeezed lime juice
2 teaspoons Worcestershire sauce
1 teaspoon Asian chile sauce
1 tablespoon very finely minced ginger
2 tablespoons minced cilantro sprigs
½ teaspoon salt

PREPARATION

In a small bowl, combine all the ingredients. Taste and adjust the seasoning. Cover and refrigerate for up to 5 days. Great for most grilled and smoked seafood.

Krazy Ketchup

2 tablespoons olive oil
1 yellow onion, chopped
10 cloves garlic, finely minced
2 tablespoons finely minced ginger
¼ cup chopped cilantro sprigs
2 tablespoons minced fresh thyme leaves
3 cups dry red wine
1½ cups ketchup
¼ cup Heinz 57 sauce
3 tablespoons Worcestershire sauce
3 tablespoons packed brown sugar
3 tablespoons chile powder
1 tablespoon molasses
1 tablespoon dried oregano
1 tablespoon sweet paprika
2 teaspoons Asian chile sauce

PREPARATION

In a 2½-quart saucepan, combine the oil and onion. Place over medium-low heat and cook until the onion is translucent, about 8 minutes. Add the garlic and ginger and sauté for 30 seconds. Add all the remaining ingredients. Bring to a low boil, cover, and reduce the heat to a simmer. Simmer for 20 minutes. Remove the lid, turn the heat to medium high, and boil the sauce until only 3 cups remain. Transfer to a bowl, cool, and refrigerate for up to 1 month. Great for most grilled and smoked meats.

Mango Chutney

2 cups chopped mangoes, peaches, or nectarines
⅓ cup dark raisins
2 serrano chiles, finely minced, including the seeds
2 cloves garlic, finely minced
2 tablespoons finely minced ginger
¼ cup water
¼ cup cider vinegar
¼ cup packed brown sugar
2 teaspoons chile powder
½ teaspoon ground cinnamon
1 teaspoon curry powder
¼ teaspoon ground allspice
½ teaspoon salt

PREPARATION

Place all the ingredients in a nonreactive saucepan. Bring to a low boil, cover, reduce the heat to a simmer, and cook until the mixture thickens, about 20 minutes. Transfer to a bowl, let cool, and refrigerate up to 2 weeks. Great for most grilled and smoked poultry, pork, veal, and lamb.

Spicy Ginger Cucumber Relish

8 Japanese cucumbers, or 2 hothouse cucumbers
2 teaspoons salt
12-ounce bottle plain Japanese rice vinegar
1 cup sugar
2 teaspoons of your favorite chile sauce
¼ cup finely minced ginger
3 cloves garlic, finely minced

PREPARATION

Trim the ends from the cucumbers. Cut the cucumbers in half lengthwise, then cut them crosswise into ¼-inch-wide pieces. Place in a bowl, sprinkle with salt, and toss to evenly coat. After 4 hours, rinse the cucumbers. Press lightly with paper towels, then chop. Meanwhile, in a nonreactive saucepan, combine the rest of the ingredients. Bring to a boil, stirring, then let cool to room temperature. When the cucumbers have been rinsed and patted dry, stir the cucum-

bers into the pickling mixture. Refrigerate for at least 8 hours or up to 10 days. To use, drain the cucumbers and serve as a relish. Great with most grilled and smoked meats and for hamburgers.

Smoked Tomato Ketchup

6 pounds mesquite charcoal
8 ounces hickory chips
5 pounds Roma tomatoes
3 large yellow onions, sliced
¼ cup chopped garlic
1 cup packed brown sugar
2 cups apple cider vinegar
¼ cup pickling spice
6 black peppercorns, cracked
2 bay leaves
Salt and pepper to taste

ADVANCE PREPARATION

Prepare a mesquite fire. Cut tomatoes in half and shake out the seeds. With the cooking rack off the grill, lay the tomatoes skin side down on the rack, and season with salt and pepper. When the charcoal becomes gray, scatter 1 cup unsoaked hickory chips across the fire, and immediately place the rack over the fire and cover with the lid. After 5 minutes, remove the rack, set aside tomatoes, and repeat cooking process with remaining tomatoes. Remove the tomato skins. In a large pot, combine the onions, garlic, sugar, and vinegar. Place the pickling spice, pepper, and bay leaves in a cheesecloth bag, and add this to the pot. Bring to a boil and then simmer until the onions become clear, about 20 minutes. Add the tomatoes with their juice, and cook 20 minutes. Remove pot from heat, cool to room temperature, and discard the cheesecloth bag holding the spices. Purée the tomato liquid in a blender. Season with salt and pepper. Keep in the refrigerator for up to 2 months.

The combination of chopped fresh herbs and hoisin sauce forms a thick base that clings to the game hens during grilling and highlights the alluring high-note flavors of lime, ginger, and chiles. For a more intense flavor, separate the top edge of the breast skin from the meat, place about ¼ cup of the marinade under the skin, then work the marinade across the entire surface of the breast and leg meat. Even if your dinner guests decide not to eat the beautifully crisp skin, the meat will have absorbed all the flavors from the marinade. As a possible menu, accompany this dish with broiled polenta, tomato and feta cheese salad, and chocolate brownies with vanilla bean ice cream.

Game Hens with East-West Marinade

Serves 4 as an entrée

INGREDIENTS
4 rock Cornish game hens, split in half
Flavorless cooking oil to brush on the
    cooking rack

EAST-WEST MARINADE
6 cloves garlic, finely minced
2 tablespoons very finely minced ginger
Zest from 2 limes, minced
⅓ cup freshly squeezed lime juice
⅓ cup extra virgin olive oil
⅓ cup hoisin sauce
⅓ cup Chinese rice wine or dry sherry
¼ cup thin soy sauce
2 tablespoons honey
1 tablespoon Asian chile sauce
1 cup chopped mixed fresh basil leaves,
    cilantro sprigs, and mint leaves
¼ cup chopped fresh parsley
2 whole green onions, minced

ADVANCE PREPARATION
Rinse the game hens, pat dry, place in a bowl, cover, and refrigerate. Set aside the cooking oil, if grilling. Combine the marinade ingredients. Add the marinade to the game hens and coat the pieces evenly. Cover and refrigerate for at least 30 minutes or up to 8 hours. *All advance preparation may be completed up to 8 hours before you begin the final steps.*

FINAL STEPS
Just prior to cooking, remove the game hens from the refrigerator.

To Grill: If using a gas or electric grill, preheat to medium (350°). If using charcoal or wood, prepare a fire. When the gas or electric grill is preheated or the coals or wood are ash covered, brush the cooking rack with the oil, then lay the game hens, skin-side up, in the center of the rack. Cover the grill and regulate the heat so that it remains at a medium temperature. Grill the game hens for about 12 minutes on each side.

The game hens are done when the thighs register 160° on a meat thermometer. As the game hens cook, brush with the marinade.

To Smoke: Bring the game hens to room temperature, about 30 minutes. Prepare the smoker for barbecuing, bringing the temperature to 200° to 220°. Transfer the game hens to the smoker and cook for about 1 hour. The game hens are done when the juices run clear when the meat is prodded deeply with a fork. During smoking, brush with the marinade.

To Roast: Preheat the oven to 425°. Roast the game hens until the juices run clear when the meat is prodded deeply with a fork, about 30 minutes. During roasting, brush with the marinade.

To Serve: Transfer the game hens to a heated serving platter or 4 heated dinner plates and serve at once.

This recipe is a barbecue version of the classic Chinese recipe, Lemon Chicken. The sauce, which takes only seconds to heat and thicken in a saucepan, gives the game hens a glistening look and an intense lemon taste. For variations, try brushing the lemon sauce on fish as it cooks on the grill, or serve it as a dipping sauce for chilled shrimp. As a possible menu, accompany this dish with pasta speckled with parsley, watercress salad, and pineapple upside-down cake.

Game Hens with Lemon Mop and Sop

Serves 4 as an entrée

INGREDIENTS

4 rock Cornish game hens, split in half

Flavorless cooking oil to brush on the cooking rack

1 whole green onion

LEMON MOP AND SOP

1 tablespoon flavorless cooking oil

1 tablespoon minced ginger

2 cloves garlic, finely minced

½ cup freshly squeezed lemon juice

6 tablespoons sugar

¼ cup chicken stock

2 tablespoons thin soy sauce

½ teaspoon salt

2 teaspoons cornstarch

½ teaspoon Asian chile sauce

ADVANCE PREPARATION

Rinse the game hens, pat dry, place in a bowl, cover, and refrigerate. Set aside the cooking oil, if grilling. Set aside the green onion. In a small container, combine the cooking oil, ginger, and garlic, and set aside. In a small bowl, combine the remaining lemon mop and sop sauce ingredients, then cover and refrigerate. *All advance preparation may be completed up to 8 hours before you begin the final steps.*

FINAL STEPS

Just prior to cooking, remove the game hens from the refrigerator. Place a small saucepan over medium heat. Add the oil, ginger, and garlic. When the garlic sizzles, add the lemon sauce. Bring to a boil. When it thickens slightly, remove it from the heat.

To Grill: If using a gas or electric grill, preheat to medium (350°). If using charcoal or wood, prepare a fire. When the gas or electric grill is preheated or the coals or wood are ash covered, brush the cooking rack with the oil, then lay the game hens skin-side up in the center of the rack. Cover the grill and regulate the heat so that it remains at a medium temperature. Grill the game hens for about 12 minutes on each side. The game hens are done when the thighs register 160° on a meat thermometer (the juices will run clear when the meat is prodded deeply with a fork). As the game hens cook, brush on the lemon mop.

To Smoke: Bring the game hens to room temperature, about 30 minutes. Prepare the smoker for barbecuing, bringing the temperature to 200° to 220°. Transfer the game hens to the smoker and cook for about 1 hour. The game hens are done when the juices run clear when the meat is prodded deeply with a fork. During smoking, brush with the lemon mop.

To Roast: Preheat the oven to 425°. Roast the game hens until the juices run clear when the meat is prodded deeply with a fork, about 30 minutes. During roasting, brush with the lemon mop.

To Serve: Transfer the game hens to a heated serving platter or 4 heated dinner plates and serve at once, accompanied with the remaining lemon mop and sop.

In addition to game hens and chicken, we have used this marinade on roasted, grilled, or smoked rabbit, pork, veal, and lamb. As long as you omit the lemon juice, the marinade can be made in a larger quantity and stored in the refrigerator for 1 month. Just add a small amount of freshly squeezed lemon juice to the portion of the marinade you intend to use that night. As a possible menu, accompany this dish with pasta with Parmesan, orange and endive salad, and hot blueberry pie.

Game Hens with Mustard-Garlic-Rosemary Marinade

Serves 4 as an entrée

INGREDIENTS
4 rock Cornish game hens, split in half
Flavorless cooking oil to brush on the
    cooking rack

MUSTARD-GARLIC-ROSEMARY MARINADE
¼ cup chopped fresh rosemary needles
¼ cup minced shallots
5 cloves garlic, finely minced
1 tablespoon minced lemon zest
⅓ cup dry white wine
⅓ cup freshly squeezed lemon juice
⅓ cup extra virgin olive oil
⅓ cup Dijon mustard
¼ cup oyster sauce
¼ cup honey
2 teaspoons Asian chile sauce

ADVANCE PREPARATION
Rinse the game hens, pat dry, place in a bowl, cover, and refrigerate. Set aside the cooking oil, if grilling. Combine the marinade ingredients. Add the marinade to the game hens and coat the pieces evenly. Cover and refrigerate for at least 30 minutes or up to 8 hours. *All advance preparation may be completed up to 8 hours before you begin the final steps.*

FINAL STEPS
Just prior to cooking, remove the game hens from the refrigerator.

To Grill: If using a gas or electric grill, preheat to medium (350°). If using charcoal or wood, prepare a fire. When the gas or electric grill is preheated or the coals or wood are ash covered, brush the cooking rack with the oil, then lay the game hens, skin-side up, in the center of the rack. Cover the grill and regulate the heat so that it remains at a medium temperature. Grill the game hens for about 12 minutes on each side. The game hens are done when the thighs register 160° on a meat thermometer. As the game hens cook, brush with the marinade.

To Smoke: Bring the game hens to room temperature, about 30 minutes. Prepare the smoker for barbecuing, bringing the temperature to 200° to 220°. Transfer the game hens to the smoker and cook for about 1 hour. The game hens are done when the juices run clear when the meat is prodded deeply with a fork. During smoking, brush with the marinade.

To Roast: Preheat the oven to 425°. Roast the game hens until the juices run clear when the meat is prodded deeply with a fork, about 30 minutes. During roasting, brush with the marinade.

To Serve: Transfer the game hens to a heated serving platter or 4 heated dinner plates and serve at once.

Amazing Flavors for Pork and Veal

Pork and veal, with their delicate flavor and fine grain, are ideal candidates for grilling and slow-smoking. These meats are the bridge between the categories of seafood/poultry and beef/lamb. Any marinade and barbecue sauce used for seafood, poultry, beef, and lamb can be used with pork and veal. On the other hand, many beef and lamb marinades would overwhelm the subtlety of poultry and seafood, while citrus-based seafood and poultry marinades do nothing the enhance the distinct flavor and coarse grain of beef and lamb. Similar to seafood and poultry, all the tender cuts of pork and veal, such as pork tenderloin and veal chops, are great taste sensations whether grilled over direct heat for just a few minutes or slow-smoked for hours. However, tough cuts such as country-style spareribs, pork shoulder, and veal shanks require the long slow cooking of smoking to tenderize the meat. If you keep these general rules in mind, it is easy to vary marinades or choose an alternative cooking method.

Pork Loin, Tenderloin, Chops, Sausage: These cuts can be grilled or smoked. The traditional method of cooking pork until gray and dry has given way to the modern preference for serving these cuts when they are still lightly pink in the center or until an instant-read meat thermometer registers 150° to 155°. At this stage, all potential danger from trichinosis has been eliminated, and the pork tastes marvelously moist and tender. Smoking times: Loin, about 3 ½ hours; tenderloin, about 2 hours; chops, about 1 hour; sausage, about 1 hour.

Pork Spareribs, Baby Pork Back Ribs, Country-Style Spareribs, Butt, Shoulder, Hocks: Spareribs and baby pork back ribs are great grilled as long as they are cooked by the indirect method (see page 11), or slow-smoked. When the meat begins to shrink from the ends of the bones, ribs are perfectly done. Country-style spareribs, butt, shoulder, and hocks become tender only by slow-smoking. Smoking times: Spareribs, back ribs, and country-style spareribs, 3 to 4 hours; butt and shoulder, about 6 hours.

Veal Chops, Loin, Scaloppine: Chops and loins can be grilled or smoked. Serve them when they are still pink in the center, about 150° on an instant-read meat thermometer. Scaloppine, because they cook so quickly, should only be grilled. Just sear them on both sides until they lose their raw outside color, then serve immediately. Smoking times: Chops and loin, about 1¼ hours.

Veal Breast, Leg, Shank: These become tender only by slow-smoking. Smoking times: Breast, about 2 to 3 hours; shanks, about 3 to 4 hours.

Points to Remember When Grilling and Smoking Pork and Veal

- Pork and veal can be marinated for as little as 15 minutes or up to 8 hours. If marinated longer, the flavor does not noticeably improve, and if there is a vinegar or citrus juice in the marinade, or a salty ingredient such as oyster sauce or soy sauce, the meat may develop an unpleasant mushy exterior.

- You can brine tough cuts of pork and veal prior to smoking. This reduces the moisture content of the meat, retards the formation of bacteria during the slow-cooking process, and adds a brine flavor. For a basic brine mixture and brining techniques, see page 89.

- To prevent possible bacterial contamination, never brush any marinade over meat during the last 5 minutes of grilling. You can reserve a little of the marinade *prior* to marinating, and then spoon this over the meat once it has been cooked and transferred to dinner plates.

- Always grill pork and veal over medium heat.

- If the marinade has more than ¼ cup sugar or honey, grill the meat by the indirect method (see page 11) with a drip pan underneath the meat. Otherwise, the sugar or honey will cause the meat to blacken.

- One of the best methods for cooking tender cuts of pork and veal, such as tenderloins and chops, is to use a combination of cooking techniques. After marinating the meat, smoke it until it is about 15 minutes from being perfectly cooked. Then brush the meat with more marinade and finish cooking it on the grill. The meat will have acquired a fantastic smoky flavor, the outside will brown nicely, and if there is any sugar or honey in the marinade, the marinade will caramelize.

- If you want a less smoky flavor for "tough" cuts of meat such as pork butt and veal breasts, during the last third of the smoking process do the following: Remove the meat from the smoker and place on a layer of aluminum foil. Bring the sides of the foil up around the meat, add more marinade, and seal the foil shut. Transfer the meat to a preheated 275° oven and cook until the meat becomes extremely tender. Open the foil to test the meat for doneness.

*J*erk, a Jamaican spice mixture rubbed on pork that is then smoked over allspice branches, has become so well known that bottled jerk sauces are available at most supermarkets. However, homemade jerk sauces have a depth of flavor entirely missing in their commercially made cousins. We find that the addition of Dijon mustard, though not authentic, helps to bind all the other seasonings to the meat and creates even better-tasting ribs. As a possible menu, accompany this dish with sweet potato chips, buttered green and yellow beans, green salad, and banana tart.

Spareribs with Jerk Sauce

Serves 4 as an entrée

INGREDIENTS

2 sides spareribs

Flavorless cooking oil to brush on the cooking rack

JERK MARINADE

½ cup flavorless cooking oil

½ cup Grand Marnier

½ cup distilled white vinegar

½ cup dark soy sauce

½ cup Dijon mustard

¼ cup honey

2 teaspoons freshly ground black pepper

2 teaspoons freshly grated nutmeg

2 teaspoons ground allspice

1 teaspoon ground cinnamon

½ cup chopped cilantro sprigs

4 small whole green onions, minced

2 tablespoons minced fresh thyme leaves

10 cloves garlic, finely minced

¼ cup very finely minced ginger

3 Scotch bonnet chiles or 6 serrano chiles, very finely minced, including seeds

ADVANCE PREPARATION

Using your fingernail or a sharp, pointed knife, loosen the tough white membrane on the underside of the ribs; then, gripping the membrane along the bone at one edge with a paper towel, pull it away. Place the ribs in a nonreactive container. Combine the marinade ingredients and mix well. Rub the marinade over the ribs, coating them evenly. Cover and refrigerate for at least 1 hour or up to 8 hours. Set the oil aside, if grilling. *All advance preparation may be completed up to 8 hours before you begin the final steps.*

FINAL STEPS

Thirty minutes prior to cooking, remove the ribs from the container and place them on a baking sheet at room temperature.

To Grill: If using a gas or electric grill, preheat to medium (350°). If using charcoal or wood, prepare a fire. When the gas or electric grill is preheated or the coals or wood are ash covered, push the coals to the sides of the fuel bed, brush the cooking rack with the oil, then lay the ribs meaty side up in the center of the rack. Cover the grill and regulate the heat so that it remains at a medium temperature. Grill the ribs until the meat begins to shrink from the ends of the rib bones, about 45 minutes.

To Smoke: Prepare the smoker for barbecuing, bringing the temperature to 200° to 220°. Transfer the ribs to the smoker and cook for about 5 hours. The ribs are done when the meat begins to shrink away from the bone.

To Roast: Preheat the oven to 350°. Roast the ribs meaty-side up on an elevated wire rack, until the meat begins to shrink from the ends of the bones, about 1 hour.

To Serve: Cut the ribs into individual ribs. Transfer to a heated serving platter or 4 heated dinner plates and serve at once.

Hot Fires and Fuels

Charcoal Briquettes: Charcoal briquettes light easily, provide a steady heat, and are available at every market. They are made by burning sawdust and wood scraps in the absence of oxygen so that the wood is reduced to carbon. The carbon is then compressed into briquettes along with ground coal and binders. Many manufacturers add petroleum products and sodium nitrate, which will affect the taste of the food. Look for briquette packages that are labeled "all natural."

Lump Hardwood Charcoal: Also called "chunk hardwood," this is made by burning hardwood in a closed container without oxygen until the wood turns to carbon. It retains the irregular shape of the original pieces of wood. The advantages of lump hardwood charcoal are that it contains no additives and adds a wonderful flavor to food. However, because it burns hotter than briquettes, it is very easy to burn food, and it also sparks quite dramatically. Successful grilling using lump hardwood takes practice.

Hardwood: No other type of fuel provides food with such an alluring flavor. But cooking over hardwood takes practice and constant attention. Hardwood burns unevenly, and unlike lump hardwood charcoal and briquettes, its temperature can quickly fall below the ideal grilling heat. Always use hardwood and never softwood. Softwood has high levels of sap, which causes a harsh smoke that adds an off taste to food. We like combining small amounts of hardwood with charcoal to gain added flavor. Hardwood choices include apple, cherry, hickory, maple, mesquite, oak, and pecan.

Wood Chips, Dried Herbs, Grape Cuttings, Wine Barrel Staves: These are not used as primary heat sources. Instead, they are placed on briquettes, charcoal, hardwood, or over gas flames in order to provide additional flavor to food. If you choose hardwood lumber scraps, be sure the wood is *untreated*. Treated wood, such as wood sprayed with a wood preservative, is highly toxic. To use wood chips, see "Hot Grilling Techniques," page 10. Barrel stave chips are available at some hardware stores and through Williams-Sonoma.

Laying and Starting the Fire

Nothing is more frustrating when grilling than having to finish cooking food in the oven because the fire died. Always err on the side of building too large a fire. We use the following system, which provides a bed of coals for several days of grilling. Place a 4-inch layer of briquettes or lump charcoal over the entire surface of the fuel bed. Once the goals glow evenly, with no black areas, close all the vents halfway and cover the grill. At this point the fire will be much too hot for grilling. Wait about 5 minutes. The diminished oxygen will cause the fire to cool. Remove the top when the coals are covered with ash and you can hold your hand 4 inches from the heat for a count of "1001, 1002, 1003" before having to remove your hand. Now the fire will be at medium heat, which is the right temperature for cooking. As soon as the food is removed from the grill, cover the grill and close *all* the vents. The lack of oxygen will cause the fire to die. The next time you light the coals, the fire will quickly become evenly hot. If the fire is too hot, then repeat the procedure of closing all the vents halfway, covering the grill, and waiting about 5 minutes.

Presoaked Charcoal Briquettes: Don't use instant-lighting charcoal briquettes. These are soaked with lighter fluid, which will adversely affect the taste of the food.

Lighter Fluid: If you use just a light sprinkling of lighter fluid, it will burn off as the coals heat and will not give food a "lighter fluid" taste. Mound the charcoal into a peak and spray with lighter fluid. Place the lighter fluid can at least 10 feet away from the grill, then light the charcoal. Never reapply the lighter fluid to coals that have already been lighted. Fire can travel instantly up the stream of lighter fluid and cause the container to explode.

Kindling: Criss-cross dry sticks on top of crumbled newspaper, add the charcoal in a mound, then light the newspaper.

Electric Starters: Horseshoe-shaped electric starters work very well. Place the starter in the center of the fuel bed, add a mound of charcoal on top, then plug the cord into an electric outlet. In approximately 10 minutes, all the coals lying on top of the starter will have lighted. At this point be sure to remove the electric starter or the fire will melt the plastic handle. If this occurs, the electric starter is no longer safe to use and must be discarded. Because the electric starter coil will be extremely hot, when you remove it from the grill place it on an elevated heat-proof shelf away from children, bare feet, and animals.

Metal Chimney: Legions of backyard barbecue chefs love this device. Place one piece of crumpled newspaper in the bottom of the chimney, add charcoal, and then light the newspaper. In 20 minutes all the charcoal will have turned into glowing coals. With your hand in a heat-proof mitt, carefully lift out the chimney, letting the lighted charcoal spill across the surface of the fuel bed. Getting a large bed of coals evenly lighted takes a total of about 40 minutes when using the metal chimney. Once the lighted coals have been spilled across the grate, scatter on more charcoal. It will take about 20 more minutes for all the coals to become evenly heated.

Fire Log Starters: Never use fire-log starters. They have many chemical additives.

We couldn't resist giving a variation of this recipe, which has appeared in many of our cookbooks. The richness in taste, range of flavors, and fantastic aroma of the ribs as they cook always creates a feeding frenzy and pleading requests for the recipe. Of course, the recipe is your secret family recipe, and must never be divulged. The sauce can be made in much larger amounts and stored indefinitely in the refrigerator. As a possible menu, accompany this dish with corn bread muffins, asparagus and golden beet salad, and hot apple pecan pie.

All-Star Asian Baby Pork Back Ribs

Serves 4 as an entrée

INGREDIENTS

4 slabs baby pork back ribs, 8 ribs each

Flavorless cooking oil to brush on the cooking rack

ALL-STAR ASIAN BARBECUE SAUCE

1 cup hoisin sauce

½ cup plum sauce

⅓ cup oyster sauce

¼ cup red wine vinegar

¼ cup honey

2 tablespoons dark soy sauce

2 tablespoons dry sherry

1 tablespoon dark sesame oil

1 tablespoon Asian chile sauce

½ teaspoon five-spice powder

1 tablespoon grated or finely minced orange zest

10 cloves garlic, very finely minced

¼ cup very finely minced ginger

½ cup finely minced green onion

ADVANCE PREPARATION

Using your fingernail or a sharp, pointed knife, loosen the tough white membrane on the underside of the ribs; then, gripping the membrane along the bone at one edge with a paper towel, pull it away. Place the ribs in a nonreactive container. Set the oil aside, if grilling. Combine all ingredients for the barbecue sauce and mix well. Rub over the ribs, coating them evenly. Cover and refrigerate for at least 30 minutes or up to 4 hours. *All advance preparation may be completed up to 4 hours before you begin the final steps.*

FINAL STEPS

Thirty minutes prior to cooking, remove the ribs from the container and place them on a baking sheet at room temperature.

To Grill: If using a gas or electric grill, preheat to medium (350°). If using charcoal or wood, prepare a fire. When the gas or electric grill is preheated or the coals or wood are ash covered, push the coals to the sides of the fuel bed, brush the cooking rack with the oil, then lay the ribs meaty side up in the center of the rack. Cover the grill and regulate the heat so that it remains at a medium temperature. Grill the ribs until the meat begins to shrink from the ends of the rib bones, about 45 minutes. During grilling, brush with more of the marinade.

To Smoke: Prepare the smoker for barbecuing, bringing the temperature to 200° to 220°. Transfer the ribs to the smoker and cook for about 5 hours. The ribs are done when the meat begins to shrink away from the bone.

To Roast: Preheat the oven to 350°. Roast the ribs meaty side up on an elevated wire rack, until the meat begins to shrink from the ends of the bones, about 1 hour. During roasting, brush with more of the marinade.

To Serve: Cut the ribs into individual ribs. Transfer to a heated serving platter or 4 heated dinner plates and serve at once.

This cure, which is based on a recipe contributed by Stephen Pyles, chef/owner of the spectacular Star Canyon Restaurant in Dallas, should be rubbed across the spareribs 8 to 24 hours prior to cooking. First, the coriander and peppercorns are toasted to heighten their flavors, then they are ground finely and blended with chipotle chiles, garlic, and other spices. The very assertive flavors of the cure, which cause little "explosions" in the mouth, need an accompanying fruit salsa, such as the Fruit Salsa on page 54. Or, for a simpler presentation, serve the spareribs with sliced ripe papaya. As a possible menu, accompany this dish with jicama salad, corn bread, and homemade peach ice cream.

Spareribs with Chipotle-Coriander Cure

Serves 4 as an entrée

INGREDIENTS

2 sides spareribs

Flavorless cooking oil to brush on the
    cooking rack

CHIPOTLE-CORIANDER CURE

¼ cup coriander seeds

¼ cup black peppercorns

8 cloves garlic, peeled

4 shallots, peeled

¼ cup chipotle chiles in adobo sauce

1 cup ketchup

¼ cup molasses

¼ cup dark soy sauce

¼ cup cider vinegar

6 tablespoon packed dark brown sugar

1 tablespoon finely minced orange zest

Fruit Salsa, page 54

ADVANCE PREPARATION

Using your fingernail or a sharp, pointed knife, loosen the tough white membrane on the underside of the ribs; then, gripping the membrane along the bone at one edge with a paper towel, pull it away. Place the ribs in a nonreactive container. Set the oil aside, if grilling.

Prepare the cure: Place the coriander and peppercorns in a small dry sauté pan over medium heat and toast until the peppercorns begin to smoke. Transfer to a spice grinder and grind finely. Mince the garlic and shallots in a food processor. Add the ground spices and chipotle chiles and mince for 10 seconds. Add all the remaining cure ingredients and process until it becomes a thick paste. (Makes 2 and ½ cups.) Rub the cure over the ribs on both sides. Cover and refrigerate for at least 1 hour or up to 24 hours. *All advance preparation may be completed up to 24 hours before you begin the final steps.*

FINAL STEPS

Within 4 hours of serving, prepare the fruit salsa. Thirty minutes prior to cooking, remove the ribs from the container and place them on a baking sheet at room temperature.

To Grill: If using a gas or electric grill, preheat to medium (350°). If using charcoal or wood, prepare a fire. When the gas or electric grill is preheated or the coals or wood are ash covered, push the coals to the sides of the fuel bed, brush the cooking rack with the oil, then lay the ribs meaty side up in the center of the rack. Cover the grill and regulate the heat so that it remains at a medium temperature. Grill the ribs until the meat begins to shrink from the ends of the rib bones, about 45 minutes.

To Smoke: Prepare the smoker for barbecuing, bringing the temperature to 200° to 220°. Transfer the ribs to the smoker and cook for about 5 hours, or until the meat begins to shrink away from the bones.

To Roast: Preheat the oven to 350°. Roast the ribs meaty side up on an elevated wire rack, until the meat begins to shrink from the ends of the bones, about 1 hour.

To Serve: Cut into individual ribs. Transfer to a heated serving platter or 4 heated dinner plates and serve at once with the fruit salsa.

This glaze is a variation of an apricot dipping sauce that we often use for chilled shrimp, spring rolls, and deep-fried wontons. The glaze gains its intense apricot flavor from dried apricots that are simmered in a sweet-sour apricot nectar mixture until tender, then puréed. Large amounts of minced ginger, chopped cilantro, and Asian chile sauce contribute exciting flavor contrasts as the glaze is brushed repeatedly over the pork tenderloin during cooking. If you delete the cilantro, the glaze can be stored indefinitely in the refrigerator. Just add the cilantro to the portion of the glaze you plan to use that day. As a possible menu, accompany this dish with wild rice with pine nuts, brussels sprouts, field green salad, and ginger crème brûlée.

Pork Loin with
Spicy Apricot Glaze ———————————————— *Serves 4 as an entrée*

INGREDIENTS
1 ½ pounds pork loin

Flavorless cooking oil to brush on the
cooking rack

SPICY APRICOT GLAZE
16 dried apricots

1 ½ cups (12 ounces) apricot nectar

¾ cup sugar

½ cup distilled white vinegar

½ cup water

1 tablespoon Asian chile sauce

1 teaspoon salt

⅓ cup finely minced ginger

3 cloves garlic, minced

2 tablespoons white sesame seeds

2 whole green onions, minced

¼ cup minced cilantro sprigs

ADVANCE PREPARATION
Trim off and discard any excess fat from the pork, then cover and refrigerate the pork. Set aside the cooking oil, if grilling. In a small nonreactive saucepan, combine the apricots, nectar, sugar, vinegar, water, chile sauce, salt, ginger, and garlic. Bring to a low boil, reduce the heat to a simmer, cover, and cook for 30 minutes. Let cool to room temperature, then purée in a blender until completely smooth. Transfer to a bowl. Place the sesame seeds in a dry skillet and toast over medium heat until golden. Add the sesame seeds, green onions, and cilantro to the apricot glaze. If not using right away, cover and refrigerate. *All advance preparation may be completed up to 8 hours before you begin the final steps.*

FINAL STEPS
One hour prior to cooking, place the loin in a nonreactive container, add half the apricot glaze, and turn the pork to coat evenly. The remaining apricot glaze will become the sauce. Let sit at room temperature.

To Grill: If using a gas or electric grill, preheat to medium (350°). If using charcoal or wood, prepare a fire. When the gas or electric grill is preheated or the coals or wood are ash covered, brush the cooking rack with the oil, then lay the pork in the center of the rack. Cover the grill and regulate the heat so that it remains at a medium temperature. Grill the pork until an instant-read meat thermometer registers 160° when inserted deeply into the meat, about 20 to 30 minutes. During cooking, brush on more of the apricot glaze.

To Smoke: Prepare the smoker for barbecuing, bringing the temperature to 200° to 220°. Transfer the pork to the smoker and cook for about 4 hours, or until the pork reaches an internal temperature of 160°. As it smokes, brush with more apricot glaze.

To Roast: Preheat the oven to 350°. Roast the pork until the internal temperature reaches 160°, about 1 hour. During roasting, brush with more of the apricot glaze.

To Serve: Let the pork rest for 10 minutes. Spoon the apricot sauce onto a heated serving platter or 4 heated dinner plates. Slice the pork and arrange it on top of the sauce. Serve at once.

Tom Young, chef and owner at Expressions Restaurant in the North Carolina hill town of Hendersonville, contributed this barbecue sauce. It adds a great taste when brushed across any cut of poultry, lamb, beef, or pork as it cooks on the grill or in the smoker. Please note: pork shoulder is a tough cut of meat that must be slow-cooked for hours to become tender, so there are no directions provided for grilling or oven-roasting. As a possible menu, accompany this dish with warm flour tortillas, tomato and feta salad, and blueberry crisp with vanilla bean ice cream.

Southern Pulled Pork

Serves 8 to 10 as an entrée

INGREDIENTS

4- to 5-pound pork shoulder

¼ cup chile powder

1 teaspoon crushed red pepper flakes

1 tablespoon ground black pepper

1 tablespoon packed brown sugar

1 teaspoon dried thyme

CAROLINA MOUNTAIN BARBECUE SAUCE

1 medium yellow onion

4 cloves garlic, finely minced

1 cup packed brown sugar

2 cups ketchup

¾ cup apple cider vinegar

½ cup thin soy sauce

2 tablespoons Worcestershire sauce

1 teaspoon crushed red pepper flakes

1 teaspoon dry mustard

1 tablespoon finely minced pepper

Fruit Salsa, page 54

ADVANCE PREPARATION

Trim the excess fat from the sides of the meat. Place the pork in a nonreactive container.

In a small bowl, combine the chile powder, crushed red pepper, black pepper, brown sugar, and thyme and mix well. Rub over the entire surface of the meat. If not smoking the pork within 1 hour, refrigerate for at least 1 hour or up to 24 hours.

Prepare the barbecue sauce: Cut the onion into ¼-inch slices. Place in a stovetop smoker and smoke over hickory dust for about 10 minutes. Alternatively, grill or broil the onion slices until dark golden. Transfer the onion to a saucepan and add the remaining barbecue sauce ingredients. Bring to a simmer, reduce heat to low, cover, and simmer for 30 minutes. Pour the sauce through a medium-meshed strainer, scraping the sieve with a metal spoon to force all the pulp through the sieve. Cover and refrigerate the sauce. *All advance preparation may be completed up to 24 hours before you begin the final steps.*

FINAL STEPS

Prepare the salsa; cover and refrigerate. One hour prior to cooking, remove the pork from the refrigerator. Reserve half the sauce to serve with the cooked meat.

To Smoke: Prepare the smoker for barbecuing, bringing the temperature to 200° to 220°. Place the meat in the smoker and cook for about 1 ½ hours per pound, or until the internal temperature reaches 170° to 180° on an instant-read meat thermometer. Every 30 minutes, brush the meat with the sauce.

To Serve: Remove the meat from the smoker and let sit 15 minutes. Then pull the meat into chunks or shreds and transfer it to a heated serving platter or heated dinner plates. Serve accompanied with the reserved sauce and the fruit salsa.

The juice from blood oranges contributes a striking color to any sauce. Grown mostly in Florida and available only during the winter-spring season at upscale supermarkets across the country, blood oranges have a partially red exterior and a reddish-black flesh. Rather than freezing the juice, which will cause it to deteriorate in flavor, when blood oranges are unavailable substitute regular orange juice, or freshly squeezed tangerine juice. As a possible menu, accompany this dish with garlic mashed potatoes with chive blossoms, watercress salad, and flourless chocolate cake.

Pork Tenderloin with Blood Orange Sauce

Serves 4 as an entrée

INGREDIENTS

2 pork tenderloins, each about
    12 ounces
Flavorless cooking oil to brush on the
    cooking rack

CUMIN RUB

2 teaspoons ground cumin
1 teaspoon ground cinnamon
1 teaspoon sweet paprika
½ teaspoon cayenne pepper
1 teaspoon salt

BLOOD ORANGE SAUCE

1 tablespoon cornstarch
2 tablespoons olive oil
3 cloves garlic, finely minced
1 cup freshly squeezed blood orange,
    regular orange, or tangerine juice
½ cup dry white wine
2 tablespoons honey
1 teaspoon Asian chile sauce
½ teaspoon salt
¼ cup slivered fresh basil leaves
¼ cup chopped cilantro sprigs
1 teaspoon Cumin Rub, above

ADVANCE PREPARATION

Place the pork in a nonreactive container. Set aside the cooking oil, if grilling. In a small bowl, combine the cumin rub ingredients. Stir well, then rub all but 1 teaspoon of the cumin rub evenly over the pork, cover, and refrigerate for at least 30 minutes or up to 24 hours. Set aside the cornstarch. In a small bowl, combine the olive oil and garlic. In another bowl, combine all the remaining sauce ingredients, stirring in the remaining 1 teaspoon of the cumin rub. *All advance preparation may be completed up to 24 hours before you begin the final steps.*

FINAL STEPS

Thirty minutes prior to cooking, remove the meat from the refrigerator.

To Grill: If using a gas or electric grill, preheat to medium (350°). If using charcoal or wood, prepare a fire. When the gas or electric grill is preheated or the coals or wood are ash covered, brush the cooking rack with the oil, then lay the pork in the center of the rack. Cover the grill and regulate the heat so that it remains at a medium temperature. Grill the pork until an instant-read meat thermometer registers 150° when inserted deeply into the meat, about 20 minutes.

To Smoke: Prepare the smoker for barbecuing, bringing the temperature to 200° to 220°. Transfer the pork to the smoker and cook for about 2 hours, or until the meat reaches an internal temperature of 150°.

To Roast: Preheat the oven to 350°. Roast the pork until the internal temperature reaches 150°, about 30 minutes.

To Serve: Combine the cornstarch with 1 tablespoon cold water. Place a 12-inch sauté pan over high heat and add the olive oil and garlic. When the garlic sizzles but has not browned, add the blood orange sauce. Bring to a rapid boil. Stir in just enough cornstarch mixture to lightly thicken the sauce. Taste and adjust the seasoning. Spoon the sauce onto a heated serving platter or 4 heated dinner plates. Slice the pork and arrange the pieces on top of the sauce. Serve at once.

This recipe is contributed by Kim David, one of Napa's most passionate cooks. Be sure to ask the butcher to scrape the long rib bones completely clean of fat, a process called frenching. The lamb should be marinated for at least 2 hours, but it will be even better if marinated up to 8 hours. For variations, use the marinade on chicken pieces, or add ¹/₄ cup chopped cilantro, basil, or rosemary to the marinade. As a possible menu, accompany this dish with garlic bread, asparagus salad with roasted red peppers, and vanilla bean cheesecake.

Balsamic-Soy Rack of Lamb

Serves 4 as an entrée

INGREDIENTS

2 racks of lamb

Flavorless cooking oil to brush on the cooking rack

2 tablespoons mixed red, green, white, and black peppercorns

½ cup Swedish mustard or honey mustard

BALSAMIC SOY MARINADE

¾ cup balsamic vinegar

¾ cup dry red wine

½ cup dark soy sauce

¼ cup Dijon or honey mustard

10 cloves garlic, finely minced

ADVANCE PREPARATION

Remove all outside fat from the lamb and trim the fat and meat between the bones down to the loin. Using a thin-bladed knife, make a small cut along the backbone between each of the bones so that the meat is slightly pierced. Place the lamb in a non-reactive container. Set aside the cooking oil, if grilling. Place the peppercorns in a sauté pan over medium heat, and toast until the peppercorns begin to "pop" and "hop." Transfer the peppercorns to a spice grinder or mortar and coarsely grind. Set aside the mustard. In a small bowl, combine all the marinade ingredients. Stir, then pour over the lamb. Work the marinade into the meat slashes, then cover, and refrigerate for at least 2 or up to 8 hours. *All advance preparation may be completed up to 8 hours before you begin the final steps.*

FINAL STEPS

One hour prior to cooking, remove the lamb from the refrigerator. Rub the lamb with the pepper mix, then rub it with the honey mustard.

To Grill: If using a gas or electric grill, preheat to medium (350°). If using charcoal or wood, prepare a fire. When the gas or electric grill is pre-heated or the coals or wood are ash covered, brush the cooking rack with the oil, then lay the lamb in the center of the rack. Cover the grill and regulate the heat so that it remains at a medium temperature. Grill the lamb until the internal temperature registers 140° when an instant-read meat thermometer is inserted into the center of the meat, about 17 to 20 minutes. The lamb will be medium rare.

To Smoke: Prepare the smoker for barbecuing, bringing the temperature to 200° to 220°. Transfer the lamb to the smoker and cook for about 2 hours, or until the lamb reaches an internal temperature of 140°.

To Roast: Preheat the oven to 450°. Roast the lamb until the internal temperature reaches 140°, about 20 minutes.

To Serve: Remove the lamb from the heat and let rest for 5 minutes. Cut each rack in half. Transfer to a heated serving platter or 4 heated dinner plates and serve at once.

O ne of our most popular recipes is chicken wings marinated for 24 hours in a rich Asian mix of condiments, spices, and herbs, then roasted in a 375° oven for 1 hour. The following recipe uses a slightly different marinade combination for lamb kabobs by increasing the amount of chile sauce and adding chopped cilantro and finely minced ginger. Marinate the lamb for 8 hours, if possible, so the flavors permeate the meat, and brush on more of the marinade often during the grilling. As a possible menu, accompany this dish with hot and sour soup, pineapple fried rice, and mango ice cream with chocolate sauce.

Mahogany Lamb Kabobs —————————— Serves 4 as an entrée

INGREDIENTS

1½ pounds lamb leg meat, trimmed of all fat

12 metal skewers, each 8 inches long

Flavorless cooking oil to brush on the cooking rack

MAHOGANY MARINADE

1 cup hoisin sauce

¾ cup plum sauce

½ cup thin soy sauce

⅓ cup red wine vinegar

¼ cup Chinese rice wine or dry sherry

¼ cup honey

2 teaspoons Asian chile sauce

4 whole green onions, minced

½ cup chopped cilantro sprigs

6 large cloves garlic, finely minced

2 tablespoons finely minced ginger

ADVANCE PREPARATION

Cut the lamb into 1 inch cubes. Thread the cubes onto the skewers and place in a nonreactive container. Set aside the cooking oil, if grilling. In a bowl, combine all the marinade ingredients and mix well. Pour the marinade over the meat, coat evenly, cover, and refrigerate at least 1 hour or for up to 8 hours. *All advance preparation may be completed up to 8 hours before you begin the final steps.*

FINAL STEPS

One hour prior to cooking, remove the lamb from the refrigerator.

To Grill: If using a gas or electric grill, preheat to medium (350°). If using charcoal or wood, prepare a fire. When the gas or electric grill is preheated or the coals or wood are ash covered, brush the cooking rack with the oil, then lay the lamb in the center of the rack.

Regulate the heat so that it remains at a medium temperature. Grill the kabobs until they are brown on the outside and medium rare in the center, about 15 minutes (cut into one). During grilling, brush with the marinade.

To Smoke: Prepare the smoker for barbecuing, bringing the temperature to 200° to 220°. Transfer the lamb to the smoker and cook for about 45 minutes, or until brown on the outside and medium rare in the center.

To Broil: Preheat the broiler. Broil the lamb 4 inches from the heat source for about 12 minutes, or until brown on the outside and medium rare in the center. Turn the kabobs midway through the cooking and brush on more marinade.

To Serve: Remove the lamb from the heat. Transfer the skewers to a heated serving platter or 4 heated dinner plates and serve at once.

We have stored this marinade for months in the refrigerator without any deterioration in flavor. It's especially good on poultry, pork, lamb, and beef. When planning to make this recipe, be sure to ask the butcher to trim off all exterior fat from the tenderloin, but do not have the butcher tie the tenderloin into a single, evenly thick strip. We think it is much better to separate the tenderloin into its natural muscle formation, and to separately cook these different-sized pieces. This way everyone gets meat done to their preference, and there are more delicious end pieces to nibble on. As a possible menu, accompany this dish with garlic mashed potatoes, grilled summer squash, salad of baby greens, and fresh berries and chocolates.

Chinois Beef Tenderloin

Serves 4 as an entrée

INGREDIENTS

1 piece of beef tenderloin, about 2 pounds

Flavorless cooking oil to brush on the cooking rack

CHINOIS BARBECUE SAUCE

1¼ cup hoisin sauce

¾ cup dry red wine

½ cup lightly flavored olive oil

½ cup Dijon mustard

3 tablespoons dark soy sauce

1 tablespoon Asian chile sauce

12 cloves garlic, finely minced

½ cup fresh rosemary needles, minced

ADVANCE PREPARATION

Trim the meat of all exterior fat. Separate the tenderloin into its individual muscle formations, making about 3 pieces. Place the beef in a nonreactive container. Set aside the cooking oil, if grilling. In a small bowl, combine all the barbecue sauce ingredients. Pour the sauce over the beef to coat evenly, cover, and refrigerate for at least 1 hour or up to 8 hours. *All advance preparation may be completed up to 8 hours before you begin the final steps.*

FINAL STEPS

One hour prior to cooking, remove the steak from the refrigerator.

To Grill: If using a gas or electric grill, preheat to medium (350°). If using charcoal or wood, prepare a fire. When the gas or electric grill is preheated or the coals or wood are ash covered, brush the cooking rack with the oil, then lay the beef in the center of the rack. Cover the grill and regulate the heat so that it remains at a medium temperature. Grill the beef until the internal temperature registers 140° when an instant-read thermometer is inserted into the center of the meat, about 25 minutes. The meat will be medium rare. During grilling, brush with the barbecue sauce.

To Smoke: Prepare the smoker for barbecuing, bringing the temperature to 200° to 220°. Transfer the beef to the smoker and cook for about 1 ½ hours, or until the beef reaches an internal temperature of 140°. During smoking, brush with the barbecue sauce.

To Roast: Preheat the oven to 450°. Roast until the internal temperature of the beef reaches 140°, about 30 minutes. During roasting, brush with the barbecue sauce.

To Serve: Remove the beef from the heat and let rest for 5 minutes before cutting into steaks. Transfer to a heated serving platter or 4 heated dinner plates and serve at once.

There are few better taste sensations than a perfect hamburger. Freshly ground chuck should be formed by hand into patties, grilled, and served with perfectly toasted sourdough sesame seed buns, sliced vine-ripened tomatoes, crisp lettuce, various condiments, and pickles. Our All-Star Asian Barbecue Sauce, brushed on the hamburgers as they cook, adds a fantastic flavor. The recipe specifies ground chuck because it has more flavor and is more moist than ground beef from sirloin (which is tender but less flavorful) or from ground tri-tip and flank steak (lots of flavor but too lean). It's the 22% fat content of ground chuck that keeps the meat so moist during grilling.

Asian Burgers

Serves 4 as an entrée

INGREDIENTS

Flavorless cooking oil to brush on
    the cooking rack

1½ pounds ground beef chuck
    (22% fat)

3 tablespoons ketchup

2 tablespoons oyster sauce

3 cloves garlic, minced

1 tablespoon very finely minced
    ginger

¼ teaspoon finely minced
    orange zest

1 whole green onion, finely minced

All Star Asian Barbecue Sauce,
    page 67

4 hamburger buns

Sliced vine-ripened tomatoes

Lettuce

Mayonnaise

ADVANCE PREPARATION

Set oil aside, if grilling. Place the beef in a mixing bowl. Add the ketchup, oyster sauce, garlic, ginger, zest, and green onion. Using your fingers, mix thoroughly. Form the meat into 4 equal-sized balls, then flatten gently with your palm. Cover and refrigerate. Prepare the barbecue sauce. Reserve 1 cup of the barbecue sauce for serving. Have ready the buns, tomatoes, lettuce, and mayonnaise. *All advance preparation may be completed up to 8 hours before you begin the final steps.*

FINAL STEPS

Just prior to cooking, remove the meat from the refrigerator.

To Grill: If using a gas or electric grill, preheat to medium (350°). If using charcoal or wood, prepare a fire. When the gas or electric grill is preheated or the coals or wood are ash covered, brush the cooking rack with the oil, then lay the hamburgers in the center of the rack. Regulate the heat so that it remains at a medium temperature. Grill the hamburgers for about 3 minutes on each side, until the meat is medium rare, or 4 minutes for well done, depending on your preference. During cooking, brush on the barbecue sauce.

To Broil: Preheat the broiler. Broil the hamburgers 4 inches from the heat source for about 2 minutes on each side, until the meat is medium rare, or 4 minutes for well done, depending on your preference. During cooking, brush on the barbecue sauce.

To Serve: As the hamburgers cook, toast the buns. Remove the hamburgers from the heat. Serve at once, accompanied with the sliced tomatoes, lettuce, mayonnaise, and the reserved barbecue sauce.

*A*ll too frequently, dinner parties involve insanely complicated dishes combined into baroque menus. Sadly, this rush to demonstrate culinary prowess often leads to food of varying quality, and always transforms dinners into a kind of frantic cooking competition. Our advice is serve only a few well-seasoned dishes—then you will be a culinary hero. Here's a menu that will satisfy any baseball player, baker, or banker. As a possible menu, accompany this dish with tortilla soup, Caesar salad with croutons, and strawberry milk shakes.

Southwest Burgers — *Serves 4 as an entrée*

INGREDIENTS

Flavorless cooking oil to brush on
    the cooking rack
1½ pounds ground beef chuck
    (22% fat)
4 cloves garlic, finely minced
½ cup minced shallots
1 teaspoon salt
3 ounces goat cheese
Smoked Tomato Ketchup, page 55
4 hamburger buns
Sliced vine-ripened tomatoes
1 red onion, very thinly sliced
Lettuce
Mayonnaise

ADVANCE PREPARATION

Set oil aside, if grilling. Place the beef in a mixing bowl. Add the garlic, shallots, and salt. Using your fingers, mix thoroughly. Form the meat into 4 equal-sized balls, then flatten gently with your palm. Cover and refrigerate.

Crumble the goat cheese, cover, and refrigerate. Prepare the smoked tomato ketchup. Have ready the buns, tomatoes, red onions, lettuce, and mayonnaise. *All advance preparation may be completed up to 8 hours before you begin the final steps.*

FINAL STEPS

Just prior to cooking, remove the meat from the refrigerator.

To Grill: If using a gas or electric grill, preheat to medium (350°). If using charcoal or wood, prepare a fire. When the gas or electric grill is preheated or the coals or wood are ash covered, brush the cooking rack with the oil, then lay the hamburgers in the center of the rack. Regulate the heat so that it remains at a medium temperature. Grill the hamburgers for about 3 minutes on each side, until the meat is medium rare, or 4 minutes for well done, depending on your preference.

To Broil: Preheat the broiler. Broil the hamburger 4 inches from the heat source for about 3 minutes on each side, until the meat is medium rare, or 4 minutes for well done, depending on your preference.

To Serve: As the hamburgers cook, toast the buns. Remove the hamburgers from the heat and sprinkle the top of each hamburger with the goat cheese. Serve at once, accompanied with the smoked tomato ketchup, sliced tomatoes, red onions, lettuce, and mayonnaise.

*F*lank steak has a wonderful, intense beef flavor, but does require special care so that the meat is tender. Sear flank steak on both sides, then cook it over medium-high heat only until the interior is cooked rare to medium rare. Remove the meat from the grill and let it rest at room temperature for 5 minutes. Flank steak that is cut immediately after being removed from the grill loses much of its interior moisture and will always taste tough. Now, cut the flank steak on a very sharp bias across the grain into paper-thin slices. Cut in any other manner, flank steak will taste tough. If you don't want to use flank steak, this recipe is also great made with any tender steak such as rib eye, tenderloin, T-bone, and porterhouse. As a possible menu, accompany this dish with coconut rice pilaf, cucumber-tomato salad, and passion fruit ice cream.

Smoking Thai Beef

Serves 4 as an entrée

INGREDIENTS

1 flank steak, about 1½ pounds
Flavorless cooking oil to brush on the
    cooking rack

THAI BEEF MARINADE

5 cloves garlic
1-inch piece of ginger, thinly sliced
3-inch stalk lemongrass, thinly sliced
    (optional)
3 serrano chiles, stemmed
1 cup (total) loosely packed mixed fresh
    mint leaves, basil leaves, and cilantro
    sprigs
¼ cup Chinese rice wine or dry sherry
¼ cup packed dark brown sugar
3 tablespoons flavorless cooking oil
Zest from 2 limes, finely minced
Juice from 2 limes
2 teaspoons ground coriander

ADVANCE PREPARATION

Trim any fat from the flank steak and place the steak in a nonreactive container. Set aside the cooking oil, if grilling.

Prepare the marinade: With the mincing blade in the food processor and the machine on, add to the feed tube the garlic, then the ginger, then the lemongrass, then the chiles. Mince finely. Remove the top, add the herbs, and mince finely. Add all the remaining ingredients and process for 30 seconds. Add the marinade to the meat, turn the meat to evenly combine, cover, and refrigerate. *All advance preparation may be completed up to 24 hours before you begin the final steps.*

FINAL STEPS

One hour prior to cooking, remove the steak from the refrigerator.

To Grill: If using a gas or electric grill, preheat to medium (350°). If using charcoal or wood, prepare a fire. When the gas or electric grill is preheated or the coals or wood are ash covered, brush the cooking rack with the oil, then lay the meat in the center of the rack. Cover the grill and regulate the heat so that it remains at a medium temperature. Grill the flank steak for about 4 minutes on each side, or until browned on the outside but rare in the center (cut into it).

To Smoke: Prepare the smoker for barbecuing, bringing the temperature to 200° to 220°. Transfer the flank steak to the smoker and cook about 1½ hours, removing it when still rare.

To Serve: Let the meat rest for 5 minutes. Then very thinly slice the meat across the grain on a sharp bias into very thin slices. Transfer the slices to a heated serving platter or 4 heated dinner plates and serve at once.

This is one of the more elaborate recipes in the book, but it's worth every minute of preparation! The steaks first are rubbed with a seasoning mix, then, after grilling, they're served in the center of a reduction of roasted red peppers and red wine. The roasted red pepper sauce also makes a great flavor accent for virtually anything served from the grill or smoker. As a possible menu, accompany this dish with roasted potatoes, Cobb salad, and homemade strawberry ice cream.

Sizzling Beef with *excellent* Roasted Red Pepper Sauce

Serves 4 as an entrée

INGREDIENTS

4 rib eye steaks, each ½ inch thick

3 ounces goat cheese, crumbled

½ cup cilantro sprigs

Flavorless cooking oil to brush on the cooking rack

SIZZLING BEEF RUB

4 cloves garlic, finely minced

18 allspice berries

1-inch piece cinnamon stick

1 teaspoon black peppercorns

1 teaspoon coriander seeds

½ teaspoon whole cloves

3 tablespoons chile powder

3 tablespoons packed dark brown sugar

1 tablespoon dried thyme

2 teaspoons dry mustard

1½ teaspoons salt

1 teaspoon freshly grated nutmeg

ROASTED RED PEPPER SAUCE

1 cup bottled roasted red peppers

1 cup chicken stock

1 cup dry red wine

2 tablespoons honey

2 teaspoons Asian or your favorite chile sauce

ADVANCE PREPARATION

Trim the excess fat from the edges of the steak. Place the steak in a nonreactive container. Refrigerate separately the goat cheese and cilantro. Set aside the cooking oil, if grilling.

Prepare the rub: Rub the garlic over both sides of the meat. Place the allspice, cinnamon, peppercorns, coriander, and cloves in a small dry sauté pan. Place the pan over medium heat and toast until the spices just begin to smoke, then grind finely in an electric spice grinder. In a small bowl, combine the ground spices with the rest of the rub ingredients and stir to evenly combine. Reserve 2 teaspoons of the rub. Rub the rest of the rub evenly on all sides of the meat, then cover and refrigerate for at least 1 to 8 hours.

Place all ingredients for the roasted red pepper sauce in an electric blender. Add the 2 teaspoons of the rub, then liquefy. Transfer to a small saucepan and boil over high heat until reduced to 1½ cups. Cool and refrigerate. *All advance preparation may be completed up to 8 hours before you begin the final steps.*

FINAL STEPS

One hour prior to cooking, remove the steak from the refrigerator. Mince the cilantro.

To Grill: If using a gas or electric grill, preheat to medium (350°). If using charcoal or wood, prepare a fire. When the gas or electric grill is preheated or the coals or wood are ash covered, brush the cooking rack with the oil, then lay the beef in the center of the rack. Grill the steaks until rare to medium rare, about 3 minutes on each side.

To Smoke: Prepare the smoker for barbecuing, bringing the temperature to 200° to 220°. Place the steaks in the smoker and cook for about 30 minutes, or until rare to medium rare.

To Broil: Preheat the broiler. Broil the steaks about 4 inches from the heat source until rare to medium rare, about 3 minutes on each side.

To Serve: Bring the roasted red pepper sauce to a simmer; taste and adjust the seasonings, especially for salt. Spoon the sauce onto 4 heated dinner plates. Place the meat in the center of the sauce. Sprinkle the goat cheese and cilantro over the sauce. Serve at once.

We have found this recipe is wonderful for grilled chicken and game hens, pork loins and chops, and all steaks cooked over direct heat. The amazing glaze is great as ketchup and will last indefinitely if refrigerated. As a possible menu, accompany this dish with hearts of romaine, oven-roasted potato wedges, and strawberry shortcake.

Rib Eye Steaks with Amazing Glaze

Serves 4 as an entrée

INGREDIENTS

4 rib eye steaks, each ½ inch thick

Flavorless cooking oil to brush on the cooking rack

AMAZING GLAZE

1 tablespoon olive oil

½ yellow onion, chopped

6 cloves garlic, finely minced

2 tablespoons minced fresh thyme leaves

2 cups dry red wine

1½ cups ketchup

3 tablespoons Heinz 57 Sauce

3 tablespoons packed brown sugar

2½ tablespoons dark sesame oil

2 tablespoons chile powder

1 tablespoon molasses

1 tablespoon dried oregano

1 tablespoon paprika

½ tablespoon dried sage

½ tablespoon Tabasco sauce

ADVANCE PREPARATION

Place the steaks in a nonreactive container. Make the amazing glaze: In a 2½ quart saucepan, combine the oil and onion, place over medium-low heat and cook until the onion becomes translucent, about 8 minutes. Add the garlic and sauté for 30 seconds. Add all the remaining ingredients. Bring to a low boil, cover, and reduce the heat to a simmer. Simmer 20 minutes. Remove the top, turn the heat to medium-high and boil until only 2½ cups remain. Transfer to a bowl and cool. Pour half the glaze over the meat, cover, and refrigerate 1 to 8 hours. Refrigerate remaining glaze. *All advance preparation may be completed up to 8 hours before you begin the final steps.*

FINAL STEPS

One hour prior to cooking, remove the beef and the reserved glaze from the refrigerator.

To Grill: If using a gas or electric grill, preheat to medium (350°). If using charcoal or wood, prepare a fire. When the gas or electric grill is preheated or the coals or wood are ash covered, brush the cooking rack with the oil, then lay the beef in the center of the rack. Grill the steaks about 4 minutes on each side, or until the meat is still very red in the center. As the steak cooks, brush on some of the glaze that was used as the marinade.

To Smoke: Prepare the smoker for barbecuing, bringing the temperature to 200° to 220°. Transfer the steaks to the smoker and cook for about 1 hour. During the last 15 minutes of cooking, brush the meat with some of the glaze that was used as the marinade.

To Broil: Preheat the broiler. Broil the steaks about 4 inches from the heat source for about 4 minutes on each side.

To Serve: Transfer the steaks to a heated serving platter or 4 heated dinner plates and serve at once accompanied by the reserved glaze.

There are many good variations on this recipe. The steak tastes excellent using just one kind of peppercorn, or you can increase the peppercorn variety to include brown Szechwan peppercorns. Or, instead of giving the steak a preliminary rub with Cognac, rub it with an equivalent amount of Dijon mustard or hoisin sauce. We have also substituted cilantro or mint in place of the basil in the herb butter. As a possible menu, serve this dish with homemade applesauce, sourdough rolls or biscuits, field greens salad, and berry compote.

T-Bone Pepper Steaks with Herb Butter *excellent*

— *Serves 4 as an entrée*

INGREDIENTS

4 small T-bone steaks

Flavorless cooking oil to brush on the cooking rack

3 tablespoons Cognac or Grand Marnier

3 cloves garlic, finely minced

2 teaspoons white peppercorns

2 teaspoons black peppercorns

2 teaspoons dried green peppercorns

HERB BUTTER

¼ cup unsalted butter

¼ cup chopped basil leaves

ADVANCE PREPARATION

Trim off any excess fat from around the sides of the meat. Transfer the meat to a nonreactive container. Set aside the cooking oil, if grilling. Rub the steak with the Cognac and garlic. Place the peppercorns in a small dry sauté pan and toast over medium heat until they just begin to smoke, then coarsely grind. Rub the mix evenly on both sides of the steaks; cover and refrigerate for at least 1 hour or up to 8 hours. Place the butter and basil in a food processor and process until evenly blended, then refrigerate. *All advance preparation may be completed up to 8 hours before you begin the final steps.*

FINAL STEPS

One hour prior to cooking, remove the meat from the refrigerator.

To Grill: If using a gas or electric grill, preheat to medium-high (500°). If using charcoal or wood, prepare a fire. When the gas or electric grill is preheated or the coals or wood are ash covered, brush the cooking rack with the oil, then lay the steaks in the center of the rack. Cover the grill and regulate the heat so that it remains at a medium-high temperature. Grill the steaks about 5 minutes on each side, or until the steaks are brown on the outside and rare to medium-rare in the center. During the last minute of cooking, place small dots of herb butter across the steaks.

To Smoke: Prepare the smoker for barbecuing, bringing the temperature to 200° to 220°. Transfer the meat to the smoker and cook for about 2 hours, or until the internal temperature reaches 140°. Dot with herb butter during the last 5 minutes of cooking.

To Broil: Preheat the broiler. Broil the steaks about 4 inches from the heat source for about 4 minutes on each side (cut into a steak). Dot with herb butter during the last minute of cooking.

To Serve: Transfer the steaks to a heated serving platter or 4 heated dinner plates and serve at once.

Glossary

Chiles, Ancho: These reddish-purple dried chiles have a fruity, mild spicy taste that makes them a great addition to tomato sauces and homemade chili. They are sold in all Mexican markets and some American supermarkets. Substitute: Dried mulato and pasilla chiles.

Chiles, Fresh: The smaller the chili, the hotter its taste. Over 80 percent of the "heat" is concentrated in the ribs and seeds. Because it is a tedious operation to remove the seeds from Scotch bonnet, jalapeño, and serrano chiles, we always mince the chiles including the seeds. If recipes specify seeding small chiles, just use half the amount of chiles, and mince them, including the seeds, in an electric mini-chopper. Substitute: Your favorite bottled chile sauce.

Chile Sauces: These are sauces which have chiles as their primary ingredient, not to be confused with tomato-based "chili sauces." There are countless varieties of chile sauces. To add "heat" to food, use your own favorite chile sauce and vary the amount depending on personal preference. Most of the recipes in this book specify "Asian chile sauce." Best brand: Rooster brand Delicious Hot Chili Garlic Sauce, sold in 8-ounce clear plastic jars with a green cap. Refrigerate after opening. Substitute: One or more fresh jalapeño or serrano chiles.

Chipotle Chiles in Adobo Sauce: These smoked dried jalapeños (chipotle chiles) are stewed in a tomato-vinegar-garlic sauce (adobo sauce). Chipotle chiles in adobo sauce are available in 4-ounce cans at all Mexican markets and many supermarkets. To use, purée the chiles with the adobo sauce in an electric mini-chopper. It is unnecessary to remove the seeds. Substitute: None.

Citrus Juice and Zest: Freshly squeezed citrus juice has a sparkling fresh taste completely absent in all store-bought juices. Because its flavor deteriorates quickly, always squeeze citrus juice within hours of use and keep refrigerated. For recipes that say "finely minced zest," remove the colored skin (zest) of citrus using a simple tool called a "zester," then finely mince the zest rather than trying to scrape the citrus against the rasps of a cheese grater (very time-consuming).

Coconut Milk: Adds flavor and body to sauces. Always purchase a Thai brand containing only coconut and water. Do not buy the new low-calorie or "light" coconut milk, which has a terrible taste. Stir the coconut milk before using. Best brand: Chaokoh Brand from Thailand. Once opened, store coconut milk in the refrigerator for up to 1 week, then discard. Substitute: Half-and-half.

Cooking Oil: Use any flavorless oil with a high smoking temperature, such as peanut oil, canola oil, safflower oil, and corn oil.

Crème Fraîche: This is a sour-tasting thick cream with nutty undertones. Look for it in the supermarket section where sour cream is sold. Substitute: Sour cream.

Fish sauce, Thai Fish sauce, made from fermenting fish in brine, is used in Southeast Asian cooking to add a complex flavor in much the same way that the Chinese use soy sauce. Purchase Thai or Vietnamese fish sauces, which have the lowest salt content. Best brand: Three Crab Brand, Phu Quoc Flying Lion Brand, or Tiparos Brand Fish Sauce. Substitute: Light soy sauce, although the flavor is quite different.

Five-Spice Powder: A blend of anise, fennel, cinnamon, cloves, and Szechwan pepper. It is sold at all Asian markets and at the spice section of most supermarkets.

Ginger, Fresh: These pungent and spicy "roots," grown in Hawaii, are available at all supermarkets in the produce section. Buy firm ginger with a smooth skin. It is unnecessary to peel ginger unless the skin is wrinkled. To use: Because the tough ginger fiber runs lengthwise along the root, always cut the ginger crosswise in paper-thin slices, then very finely mince it in an electric mini-chopper. Store whole ginger in the refrigerator or at room temperature for up to 1 month. Substitute: None.

Herbs, Fresh and Dried: Fresh herbs have far more flavor than their dried counterparts. The only time we use dried herbs is when they are included in dry rubs. If a fresh herb is not available, substitute another type of fresh herb, but do not substitute dried herbs.

Hoisin Sauce: A thick, sweet, spicy dark condiment made with soybeans, chiles, garlic, ginger, and sugar. Once opened, it keeps indefinitely at room temperature. Best brand: Koon Chun Hoisin Sauce.

Mustards (Dijon, Creole, honey): All types of mustards can be used interchangeably. For Dijon mustard, we prefer the Maille brand, and for Creole mustard, Zatarain's.

Olive Oil: Recipes specifying "extra virgin olive oil" benefit from the additional flavor of this intensely flavored green-tinted oil. In recipes specifying just "olive oil," or "mild" or "light" olive oil, use this type of oil when little or no olive oil taste is desired.

Oyster Sauce: Also called "oyster flavored sauce," this gives dishes a rich taste without a hint of its seafood origins. Keeps indefinitely in the refrigerator. Although it is available at every supermarket, the following best brands are available mostly at Asian markets: Sa Cheng Oyster Flavored Sauce, Hop Sing Lung Oyster Sauce, and Lee Kum Kee Oyster Flavored Sauce, Premium Brand. Substitute: None.

Plum Sauce: A chutneylike condiment made with plums, apricots, garlic, red chiles, sugar, vinegar, salt, and water. It is available canned or bottled at all Asian markets and most supermarkets. Best brand: Koon Chun. It will last indefinitely if stored in the refrigerator.

Rice Wine and Dry Sherry: We prefer the flavor of Chinese rice wine. Use a good quality Chinese rice wine or an American or Spanish dry sherry. Best brands: Pagoda Brand Shao Xing Rice Wine or Pagoda Brand Shalo Hsing Hua Tiao Chiew, or use a moderately expensive dry sherry. Substitute: dry Japanese sake or dry vermouth, but not mirin, which is sweet Japanese cooking wine.

Sesame Oil, Dark: A nutty, dark golden brown oil made from toasted crushed sesame seeds. Do not confuse dark sesame oil with American-manufactured clear-colored and tasteless sesame oil, or Chinese black sesame oil, which has a strong unpleasant taste. Dark sesame oil will last for at least 1 year at room temperature, and indefinitely in the refrigerator. Best brand: Kadoya Sesame oil.

Soy Sauce, Thin: A "watery," mildly salty liquid made from soybeans, roasted wheat, yeast, and salt. Also called "light" soy sauce. If you are concerned about sodium, reduce the quantity of soy sauce, rather than using the inferior-tasting, more expensive low-sodium brands. Best brands: Koon Chun Brand Thin Soy Sauce, or Kikkoman Regular Soy Sauce.

Soy Sauce, Dark: "Dark," "heavy," or "black" soy sauce is thin soy sauce with the addition of molasses and is used to add a rich flavor and color to sauces, stews, and soups. Never confuse "dark" soy sauce with "thick" soy sauce, sold in jars, which has a syruplike consistency and an unpleasantly strong taste. Once opened, dark soy sauce keeps indefinitely at room temperature. Best Brand: Pearl River Bridge Brand Mushroom Soy Sauce.

Spices: Convenience means that most of us use preground spices. However, the flavor of any dish will be greatly improved if you grind whole spices into a powder using an electric spice grinder. Store spices in a cool, dark pantry. Discard whole spices after 2 years, and ground spices after 1 year.

Vinegars: Wine vinegars are interchangeable in these recipes. Cider vinegar or distilled white vinegar can be used interchangeably, or you can substitute white wine vinegar. For recipes calling for balsamic vinegar, make the effort to purchase this uniquely flavored nutty and slightly sweet-tasting vinegar. Use a moderately priced balsamic vinegar ($5 for an 8-ounce bottle), available in most supermarkets. If using mild-tasting Japanese rice vinegar, use the plain, or unseasoned kind. Avoid "seasoned" or "gourmet" rice vinegar, which has sugar and salt added.

Artists' Credits

We would like to give special thanks to ceramic artist Susan Eslick of San Francisco, CA, for her bold, colorful plates and bowls appearing on pages 1, 6-7, 14-15, 26, 52, 70, 105, 106, and 108. Many thanks to artist Julie Sanders of Cyclamen Studio, Berkeley, CA, whose pieces enhance pages 29, 34, 63, 73, 79, and 95. Thanks to artist Julie Cline of Oakland, CA, whose handpainted plate appears on page 59. Kathy Erteman of New York City made the graphic plates on pages 39 and 47. Thanks also to ceramicist Aletha Soule of Sebastopol, CA, for the beautiful plates on pages 17, 73, and 102. The oil-on-canvas place mats on pages 31 and 34 are by Hillary Law.

Tantau Gallery of St. Helena, CA provided the Eigen Arts plate on page 31, the Helen Faibisch/Design plate on page 75, and the Matthew Yanchuk plate on page 92. The Out of Hand Gallery in San Francisco's Noe Valley provided the Romulus Pottery pedestal plate on page 45, the Droll Designs of New York plate on page 66, and the Tom and Sara Post of Davis, CA plates on page 99.

The Culinary Institute of America at Greystone, in St. Helena, CA, provided help with the necessary cookware for the photography. Thank you all.

Acknowledgments

Many friends helped bring this book into print and we are deeply appreciative for their support. Thank you, Ten Speed Press, particularly Phil Wood, publisher Kirsty Melville, editor Heather Garnos, publicist Cynthia Traina, and Jo Ann Deck and Dennis Hayes in special sales. Our friend and book designer, Beverly Wilson, contributed her unique vision for the book. Food stylist Carol Cole from Sebastopol, CA, added her artistry with food to many of the photos. Thank you. Jack and Dolores Cakebread provided their winery kitchen for testing many of these recipes with a small group of cooking friends. All the recipes were developed using the superb Weber barbecue equipment and Commercial Aluminum Cookware. Seattle research librarian Linda Saunto provided the background information about the history of barbecue. Many thanks to chefs Ray Breman, Tom Lambing, Stephan Pyles, Craig Schauffel (for Smoked Tomato Ketchup), and Tom Young for contributing recipes, and to great home cooks Rick and Bev Durvin for Planked Salmon with Ginger Dry Rub, Kim David for Balsamic Soy Rack of Lamb, and Joe McCrary for Rib Eye Steaks with Amazing Glaze. Finally, the recipes were evaluated by the following home cooks, who contributed many thoughtful insights: Eve Benesh, Kathleen Bergin and David Lampkin, Russ and Jan Bohne, Jo Bowen, Judy Burnstein, Bill and Lynda Casper, Megan and David Cornhill, Tobey Cotsen, Kris Cox, Kim and George David, Claire Dishman, Judith Dubrawski, Peter Feit, Suzanne Figi, Yoana Georgis, Sharie and Ron Goldfarb, Robert Gordon, Blanche and Sy Gottlieb, Kim Hartman, Joann Hecht, Donna Hodgens, Linda and Ron Johnson, Bob and Lynette Kahn, Candy and Gil Katen, Bettylu and Lou Kessler, Jeannie Komsky, Susan Krueger, Jeremy Mann, Patricia Niedfelt, Michele Nipper, Jeanne Norling, Kris Robinson, Joe Rooks, Paul and Mary Jo Shane, Ellie Shulman, Sandy Sibert, Betty Silbart, Phil Stafford, Amy and Douglas Stevens, Suzanne Vadnais, Norbert Visnesky, Kathleen Williams, Hermia Woo, and Sue Zubik.

LIQUID MEASUREMENTS

Cups and Spoons	Liquid Ounces	Approximate Metric Term	Approximate Centiliters	Actual Milliliters
1 tsp	⅙ oz	1 tsp	½ cL	5 mL
1 Tb	½ oz	1 Tb	1 ½ cL	15 mL
¼ c; 4 Tb	2 oz	½ dL; 4 Tb	6 cL	59 mL
⅓ c; 5 Tb	2 ⅔ oz	¾ dL; 5 Tb	8 cL	79 mL
½ c	4 oz	1 dL	12 cL	119 mL
⅔ c	5 ⅓ oz	1 ½ dL	15 cL	157 mL
¾ c	6 oz	1 ¾ dL	18 cL	178 mL
1 c	8 oz	¼ L	24 cL	237 mL
1 ¼ c	10 oz	3 dL	30 cL	296 mL
1 ⅓ c	10 ⅔ oz	3 ¼ dL	33 cL	325 mL
1 ½ c	12 oz	3 ½ dL	35 cL	355 mL
1 ⅔ c	13 ⅓ oz	3 ¾ dL	39 cL	385 mL
1 ¾ c	14 oz	4 dL	41 cL	414 mL
2 c; 1 pt	16 oz	½ L	47 cL	473 mL
2 ½ c	20 oz	6 dL	60 cL	592 mL
3 c	24 oz	¾ L	70 cL	710 mL
3 ½ c	28 oz	⅘ L; 8 dL	83 cL	829 mL
4 c; 1 qt	32 oz	1 L	95 cL	946 mL
5 c	40 oz	1 ¼ L	113 cL	1134 mL
6 c; 1 ½ qt	48 oz	1 ½ L	142 cL	1420 mL
8 c; 2 qt	64 oz	2 L	190 cL	1893 mL
10 c; 2 ½ qt	80 oz	2 ½ L .	235 cL	2366 mL
12 c; 3 qt	96 oz	2 ¾ L	284 cL	2839 mL
4 qt	128 oz	3 ¾ L	375 cL	3785 mL
5 qt	4 ¾ L			
6 qt	5 ½ L (or 6 L)			
8 qt	7 ½ (or 8 L)			

Conversion Charts

LENGTH

⅛ in = 3 mm
¼ in = 6 mm
⅓ in = 1 cm
½ in = 1.5 cm
¾ in = 2 cm
1 in = 2.5 cm
1 ½ in = 4 cm
2 in = 5 cm
2 ½ in = 6 cm
4 in = 10 cm
8 in = 2 cm
10 in = 25 cm

TEMPERATURES

275˚F = 140˚C
300˚F = 150˚C
325˚F = 170˚C
350˚F = 180˚C
375˚F = 190˚C
400˚F = 200˚C
450˚F = 230˚C
475˚F = 240˚C
500˚F = 250˚C

OTHER CONVERSIONS

Ounces to milliliters: multiply ounces by 29.57

Quarts to liters: multiply quarts by 0.95

Milliliters to ounces: multiply milliliters by 0.034

Liters to quarts: multiply liters by 1.057

Ounces to grams: multiply ounces by 28.3

Grams to ounces: multiply grams by .0353

Pounds to grams: multiply pounds by 453.59

Pounds to kilograms: multiply pounds by 0.45

Ounces to milliliters: multiply ounces by 30

Cups to liters: multiply cups by 0.24

Index

More Hot Cookbooks by Hugh Carpenter & Teri Sandison

Fifty bold and sophisticated yet easy stir-fry recipes seasoned with a host of exciting ingredients. Perfect ideas for fresh, healthy weeknight meals or weekend entertaining. Includes more than 50 vibrant color photos.

Fifty wild and zesty recipes that combine chicken with the distinct flavors and cuisines of the world. Discover delicious and elegant ways to serve one of the most versatile and healthy meats. More than 50 color photos provide dramatic presentation ideas.

Fifty fresh and satisfying recipes that take pasta to new and dazzling heights. Packed with easy, inventive ideas, this is the complete resource for busy cooks at all levels of experience. Includes more than 50 exciting color photos.